The Vindolanda Tablets and the Ancient Economy

Kasper Grønlund Evers

TAB. VINDOL. II.213, i-ii

BAR British Series 544
2011

Published in 2016 by
BAR Publishing, Oxford

BAR British Series 544

The Vindolanda Tablets and the Ancient Economy

ISBN 978 1 4073 0842 5

© K Grønlund Evers and the Publisher 2011

COVER IMAGE *Tab.Vindol. II.213, i-ii*
Official transliteration:
'Curtius Super Cassio suo
salutem'
'ut interpreteris
et ut hordeum commer-
cium habeant a te'
Official translation:
'Curtius Super to his Cassius, greetings.'
'- so that you may explain and so that they may get from you barley as commercial goods'

The author's moral rights under the 1988 UK Copyright,
Designs and Patents Act are hereby expressly asserted.

All rights reserved. No part of this work may be copied, reproduced, stored,
sold, distributed, scanned, saved in any form of digital format or transmitted
in any form digitally, without the written permission of the Publisher.

BAR Publishing is the trading name of British Archaeological Reports (Oxford) Ltd.
British Archaeological Reports was first incorporated in 1974 to publish the BAR
Series, International and British. In 1992 Hadrian Books Ltd became part of the BAR
group. This volume was originally published by Archaeopress in conjunction with
British Archaeological Reports (Oxford) Ltd / Hadrian Books Ltd, the Series principal
publisher, in 2011. This present volume is published by BAR Publishing, 2016.

Printed in England

PUBLISHING

BAR titles are available from:

BAR Publishing
122 Banbury Rd, Oxford, OX2 7BP, UK
EMAIL info@barpublishing.com
PHONE +44 (0)1865 310431
FAX +44 (0)1865 316916
www.barpublishing.com

Abstract

The Vindolanda Tablets are rightly famous for the insights they provide into the life of Roman auxiliaries on the province of Britain's northern frontier around the turn of the first century AD. Various authors over the years have dealt with the archaeological excavations at Vindolanda, the evidence of army organisation, daily life on the frontier, military supply, literacy, and many other subjects—sometimes several of them at once. This study is not so ambitious, however, focusing solely on the various kinds of evidence provided for economic activity in the early Roman Empire.

Accordingly, the aim is to investigate how best to comprehend the economic system attested at Vindolanda and to consider the wider implications for studies of the ancient economy in general. This is accomplished by a three-step approach: first, the nature of the Vindolandan evidence is assessed, and the state of research on both studies of the ancient economy and the economy of early Roman Britain is accounted for, so as to highlight the value of the Vindolanda Tablets and lay the ground for the interpretations which follow.

Secondly, the economic activities attested by the tablets are analysed in terms of market exchange, redistribution and reciprocity, and each category is developed to suit the unique character of the evidence. Moreover, select phenomena attested at Vindolanda are compared or contrasted with evidence from similar Roman frontier establishments in other places and periods of antiquity.

Third, a model is outlined which takes into account the different economic behaviours revealed by the tablets and attempts to fit them together into one coherent, economic system, whilst also relating the activities to questions of scale in the ancient economy; moreover, the conclusions drawn in the study are discussed and compared with those of the most important authors on the subject, and the value and potential of the findings made are put into a wider perspective.

Contents

	Preface	iv
	Figures and Illustrations	v
	Abbreviations	vi
	Introduction	1
Chapter 1	The Ancient Economy: Historiography and Theory	5
Chapter 2	The Economy of Roman Britain: Evidence and Historiography	9
Chapter 3	Market Activity: Traders and Entrepreneurs	14
Chapter 4	Redistribution: No Beer, No Bravery	25
Chapter 5	Reciprocity: The 'Social Economy' of a Military Community	34
Chapter 6	The Making of a Model: Layers and Levels of Economic Activity	42
	Epilogue	51
	Appendix	52
	Bibliography	73

Preface

Ever since writing my undergraduate thesis at University of Copenhagen in 2006, I have continued to be captivated by the ancient economy. In the first instance, this led me to write a master's dissertation on the economic significance of the evidence contained in the Vindolanda Tablets at Lancaster University, in 2009—the wonderful opportunity to stay and study at Lancaster having been provided by a longstanding exchange program between Copenhagen and Lancaster. Subsequently, I handed in yet another master's dissertation at University of Copenhagen one year later, the subject now being a New Institutional Economics analysis of Greco-Roman associations of traders and shippers.

However, it is with the greatest of joys that I have found myself able to return to the *Tabulae Vindolandenses* and my 'old' dissertation, in order to revise and expand upon it prior to publication by British Archaeological Reports. Even now, the second time around, I am still amazed by the extraordinary wealth of material contained in the tablets—and I must seize the opportunity to applaud the excavators, editors, and all others whose ongoing work over the past decades has made a study like mine possible.

Cui dono lepidum novum libellum, arida modo pumice expolitum?[1]

And finally, I would like to thank Dr Paul Hayward for all his invaluable help and advice throughout the last couple of years; in addition, I owe a debt of gratitude to Dr David Shotter for reading an early draft and providing highly useful comments on Roman Britain, and I am equally indebted to Prof. Vincent Gabrielsen for his ardent support and for encouraging me to publish this study. In closing, heartfelt thanks are also due to Ms Marianne Winther without whom this book would not have been possible, and whose faith in me continues to be an inspiration.

Any mistakes or omissions remain my own.

---

[1] Catullus, *Carmina*, I, ll. 1–2.

Figures and Illustrations

Fig. 1: *The Current Dating of the Successive Occupations at Vindolanda*   2

Fig. 2: *Number of Transactions Per Period*   3

Fig. 3: *Transactions by Find Spot, Period III*   3

Fig. 4: *Vindolanda: External Links*   46

Abbreviations

O.Bu.Njem	R. Marichal (ed.), *Les Ostraca de Bu Njem* (Tripoli, 1992).
OCD	S. Hornblower and A. Spawforth (eds), *The Oxford Classical Dictionary*, 3rd rev. edn. (Oxford, 2009).
O.Claud.	J. Bingen *et al.* (eds), *Mons Claudianus. Ostraca Graeca et Latina*, vols. I–IV (Cairo, 1992–2009).
P.Dura-Europus	C. B. Welles *et al.* (eds), *The Excavations at Dura-Europus, Final Report V, Part I: The Parchments and Papyri* (New Haven, 1959).
RIB I	R. G. Collingwood and R. P. Wright (eds), *Roman Inscriptions in Britain* (Oxford, 1965).
Tab.Luguval.	R. S. O. Tomlin (ed.), 'Roman Manuscripts from Carlisle: The Ink-Written Tablets,' in *Britannia*, 29 (1998), 31–84.
Tab.Vindol. I	A. K. Bowman and J. D. Thomas (eds), *Vindolanda: The Latin Writing-Tablets (Tabulae Vindolandenses I)*, Britannia Monograph Series No. 4 (London, 1983).
Tab.Vindol. II	A. K. Bowman and J. D. Thomas (eds), *The Vindolanda Writing-Tablets (Tabulae Vindolandenses II)* (London, 1994). The texts of these tablets may also be read online at: http://vindolanda.csad.ox.ac.uk/index.shtml
Tab.Vindol. III	A. K. Bowman and J. D. Thomas (eds), *The Vindolanda Writing-Tablets (Tabulae Vindolandenses III)* (London, 2003). The texts of these tablets may also be read online at: http://vto2.csad.ox.ac.uk
Tab.Vindol. IV.i	A. K. Bowman, J. D. Thomas and R. S. O. Tomlin (eds), 'The Vindolanda Writing-Tablets (*Tabulae Vindolandenses* IV, Part 1),' in *Britannia*, 41 (2010), 187–224.
Tab.Vindon.	M. A. Speidel (ed.), *Die römischen Schreibtafeln von Vindonissa* (Brugg, 1996).
VRR I	R. Birley, *The Early Wooden Forts: The Excavations of 1973–76 and 1985–89, with Some Additional Details from the Excavations of 1991–93*, Vindolanda Research Reports, New Series I (Hexham, 1994).
VRR III	C. van Driel-Murray *et al.*, *Preliminary Reports on the Leather, Textiles, Environmental Evidence and Dendrochronology*, Vindolanda Research Reports, New Series III (Hexham, 1993).

Introduction

Evidence for economic activities in Roman times abounds all over the former Empire in the form of excavated *fora*, shipwrecks, pot shards, coins and in a multitude of other guises—the most monumental arguably being Monte Testaccio in Rome: a hill on the outskirts of the old city made up of the remains of more than fifty million discarded *amphorae*.[1] Considering the physical stamp on their environment which the Romans left behind, it is therefore not difficult to argue that there was a lot of economic activity going on, but how are we to characterise it? How, in other words, can we best comprehend, explain and model the economic world of the Romans?

Thorough analyses of the archaeology of the Roman economy can yield some answers, but what little the Romans themselves wrote on the subject—and which has survived the rough passage of some two millennia—is mostly concerned with aristocratic life and normative views on the best way to live in accordance with Roman ideals of leisure and status. And that is exactly why the *corpus* of texts known as the Vindolanda Tablets (Latin: *Tabulae Vindolandenses*) is of such great value;[2] take for instance the following fragment which reads:

> ... I shall gladly do. As to the one hundred shingles which I have at Romanius', if you have no need of them, transport them *en route* when your wagons come from time to time, on which see that you oversee your boys lest in any way... . Greet Ingenua and ... and ...
> (2nd hand?) Farewell.
> (Back, 1st hand)
> To Gabinius ... from Bellicus(?)[3]

Although this letter is sadly incomplete, it still provides valuable bits of information and at the same time raises some interesting questions. For instance, it would seem that several civilians were present at Vindolanda; that they were conducting various kinds of business; that they were part of a wider network of people involved in the exchange of goods and services; and, by implication, that they must have had some sort of dealings with the Roman army. Why Bellicus had a hundred shingles lying around of which he had no immediate need, what business Gabinius and his dependants were into that involved regular wagon transport, and who Romanius was, we will probably never know. Moreover, were they acting as independent traders and entrepreneurs profiting from supplying the army through the institution of the market? Or were they employed as contractors? Were they 'locals' or had they arrived from afar? And how important were social relations for networks of exchange?

We cannot tell on the basis of this one fragment, but by studying the entire *corpus* of tablets, we can say quite a lot more about both who was involved, about how exchange was practised, and about the economic system of which Vindolanda was a part. Taken as a whole, the Vindolanda Tablets constitute truly invaluable evidence because they bear witness to the ordinary economic activities of a wide spectrum of Roman society, ranging from slaves over traders and soldiers to people from the lower tiers of the imperial aristocracy—texts written not for literary effect nor to propound some abstract ideal, but for everyday, practical use. Furthermore, the fact that the tablets have only come to light over the last forty years, and that most of them have been published only within the last seventeen years, forces us to reconsider the state of research on the subject, as the implications of this new data are taken into account.[4]

Keeping in mind the nature, context and bias of the Vindolanda Tablets, which will all be treated below, it is the purpose of this study to argue that the ancient economy cannot in any meaningful way be described as either primitive or modern, proto-capitalistic or socially embedded, and that the Romans exhibited an economic behaviour which allowed them to employ different exchange mechanisms in different contexts. Its aim, in other words, is to investigate the implications of the Vindolandan evidence for the modelling of Roman economic activity.

These arguments will be based on a broad enquiry into different aspects of ancient economic life: first, what can the tablets tell us about Roman economic behaviour(s) in general? Second, what can we learn about the scale of economic activities within this specific context? Third, how can we best describe the system of economic processes evident at Vindolanda? And finally, what are the wider implications of the Vindolanda Tablets for the study of the ancient economy? Traditionally, archaeologists have had a near-monopoly on supplying answers for these kinds of questions, but that is exactly why this study focuses on the tablets alone: because they provide a unique possibility of obtaining independent, textual evidence of issues otherwise viewed from a more or less exclusively 'material perspective.'

In dealing with these questions, the study falls into three parts: first, chapter one is a short introduction to the historiography and theory of the ancient economy, followed by chapter two which is a brief account of the

---

[1] Among the many discussions of Monte Testaccio, see esp. B. Ward-Perkins, *The Fall of Rome and the End of Civilisation* (Oxford, 2005), p. 91.
[2] A. K. Bowman and J. D. Thomas (eds), *Vindolanda: The Latin Writing-Tablets (Tabulae Vindolandenses I)*, Britannia Monograph Series No. 4 (London, 1983); A. K. Bowman and J. D. Thomas (eds), *The Vindolanda Writing-Tablets (Tabulae Vindolandenses II)* (London, 1994); A. K. Bowman and J. D. Thomas (eds), *The Vindolanda Writing-Tablets (Tabulae Vindolandenses III)* (London, 2003); A. K. Bowman, J. D. Thomas and R. S. O. Tomlin (eds), 'The Vindolanda Writing-Tablets (*Tabulae Vindolandenses* IV, Part 1),' in *Britannia*, 41 (2010), 187–224; cited hereafter as *Tab.Vindol.* I, *Tab.Vindol.* II, *Tab.Vindol.* III and *Tab.Vindol.* IV.i, respectively.
[3] *Tab.Vindol.* III.642, translation on p. 95.
[4] In fact, the implications of recently published material from comparable frontier forts of the Roman world need to be considered as well; see below, p. 4.

evidence for the economy of Roman Britain and a survey of the relevant historiography; second, chapters three, four and five are source-driven enquiries into different kinds of economic behaviour, namely market exchange, redistribution and reciprocity; and third and last, chapter six is a synthesis of evidence and interpretations which pulls together the results of the preceding chapters, draws conclusions and discusses the significance of the research in relation to the most recent works on the subject. It will be useful, however, to begin with a brief account of the provenance of the Vindolanda Tablets and the general issues of interpretation with which they present the researcher.

The first tablet was discovered in March 1973 during excavations at the old Roman frontier fort of Vindolanda, just south of Hadrian's Wall;[5] more followed immediately, and a steady trickle of tablets and their fragments have been uncovered in successive excavations up until the present day. These so-called 'tablets' are actually thin, postcard-sized leaves of wood, made from trees that were local to the fort in its heyday, and they were inscribed with ink in much the same way as *papyri*.[6] Employing the best of preservation-techniques and infra-red photography, it has been possible to decipher several hundred fragments dating from around the turn of the first century AD.[7]

Information on the contexts of the tablets has been gleaned from the archaeological circumstances under which they were found, and from references in the texts themselves, but almost all of them share a common provenance: tablets were a cheap, local alternative to *papyri*, and 'chance-survivors' were preserved in the damp soil of the fort in spite of being discarded, owing to the anaerobic conditions of the layers in which they were found.[8] The tablets may be grouped, moreover, according to five different phases of occupation during which they were either written, received or brought to Vindolanda. As the occupying garrisons of each period either moved out or changed the layout of the fort, they dumped their tablets in random deposits as part of the process of clearing the fort for its new occupants or re-building it (see **Fig. 1**).

Period I	c. AD 85–92. The primary fort of circa 3.5 acres; *Coh. I Tungrorum*.
Period II	c. AD 92–97/100. Enlarged fort of circa 5 acres; *Coh. I Tungrorum*, succeeded by *Coh. VIIII Batavorum*.
Period III	c. AD 97/100–105. Renovated fort; *Coh. VIIII Batavorum*.
Period IV	c. AD 105–120. Re-built fort with additional and probably legionary establishment to the west; *Coh. I Tungrorum* and others.
Period V	c. AD 120-128. Re-built fort; *Coh. I Tungrorum*.
Source:	A. Birley and J. Blake (eds), *The Excavations of 2005–2006*, Vindolanda Research Reports (Hexham, 2007), p. 3; with amendments from R. Birley, *A Roman Frontier Fort*, p. 183; and from A. R. Birley, 'Some Writing-Tablets Excavated at Vindolanda in 2001, 2002 and 2003,' in *Zeitschrift für Papyrologie und Epigraphik*, 170 (2009), 267.

Fig. 1: The Current Dating of the Successive Occupations at Vindolanda

To explain more fully, the five phases correspond to five successive periods of occupation by Germanic auxiliary cohorts (the 1st Tungrian and the 9th Batavian) starting circa AD 85, that is, after Agricola's annexation of Scotland AD 77–83 and before the withdrawal to the Tyne-Solway line in AD 87, and ending (for the purposes of this study only, though—there were several later phases, but only the first five have yielded tablets) circa AD 130. The site was on the province of Britain's northern frontier and was part of a northern zone of military occupation, garrisoned by as many as 25–30,000 auxiliaries,[9] which developed into the Stanegate Road and Hadrian's Wall during the time span in question.

Moreover, it is important to emphasise that the military nature of the evidence narrows down our focus from the Roman Empire as a whole to a sub-section of that society constituting barely one per cent of the overall population.[10] In addition, as concerns the study of specific economic activities, there is the further qualification that 'it cannot be taken for granted that the various mechanisms of [army] supply were employed by the authorities in the same proportion throughout the empire,'[11] or that we have representative illustrations of all such activities at Vindolanda.

---

[5] The geographical position of Vindolanda can be seen on the map provided in chapter six, p. 46.
[6] Indeed, the linguistic conventions employed in transcribing the tablets are almost completely identical to those of papyrology, see *Tab.Vindol.* II, p. 64.
[7] For more thorough treatments of the context of the tablets, see A. K. Bowman, *Life and Letters on the Roman Frontier* (Avon, 1994), pp. 13–18; A. R. Birley, *Garrison Life at Vindolanda: A Band of Brothers* (Stroud, 2002), pp. 22–33; and E. Birley et al., *The Early Wooden Forts: Reports on the Auxiliaries, the Writing-Tablets, Inscriptions, Brands and Graffiti*, Vindolanda Research Reports, New Series, II (Hexham, 1993), pp. 10–15. Moreover, the most recent (and readable) introduction to the history and results of the archaeological excavations at Vindolanda is R. Birley, *Vindolanda. A Roman Frontier Fort on Hadrian's Wall* (Stroud, 2009).
[8] *Tab.Vindol.* I, pp. 22–24; and R. Birley, *A Roman Frontier Fort*, pp. 43–44: the layers representing different periods of occupation had each been sealed off by a layer of turf and clay laid down as foundation for the buildings of the subsequent period, and were not waterlogged but damp and, crucially, anaerobic.
[9] S. S. Frere, *Britannia*, 3rd rev. edn (London and New York, 1987), pp. 143–44.
[10] P. Erdkamp, 'Introduction,' in P. Erdkamp (ed.), *The Roman Army and the Economy* (Amsterdam, 2002), p. 5.
[11] Quote from Erdkamp, 'Introduction,' p. 9; similar in Bowman, *Life and Letters*, p. 35.

Introduction

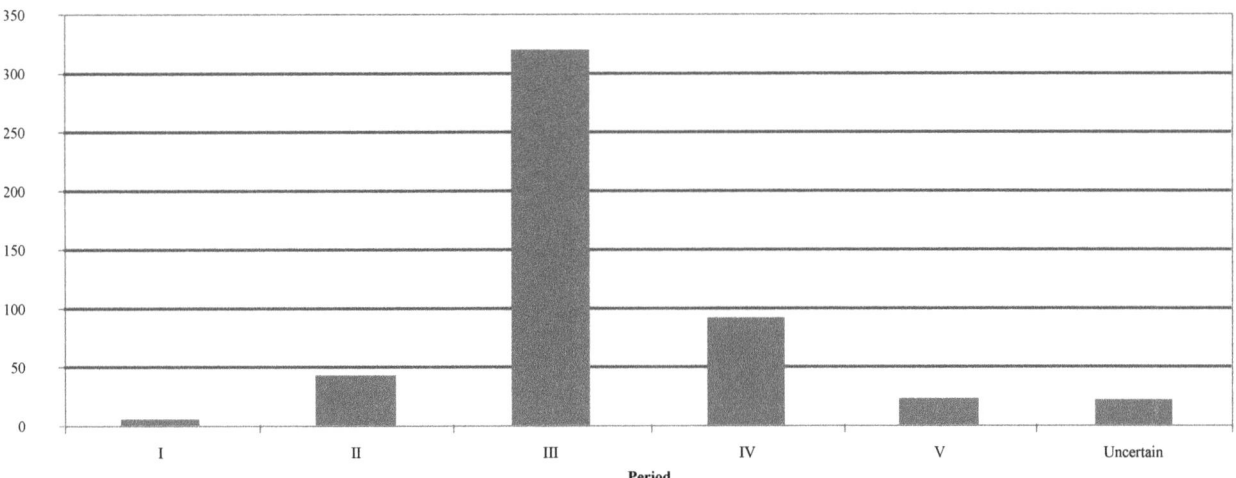

Fig. 2: Number of Transactions Per Period

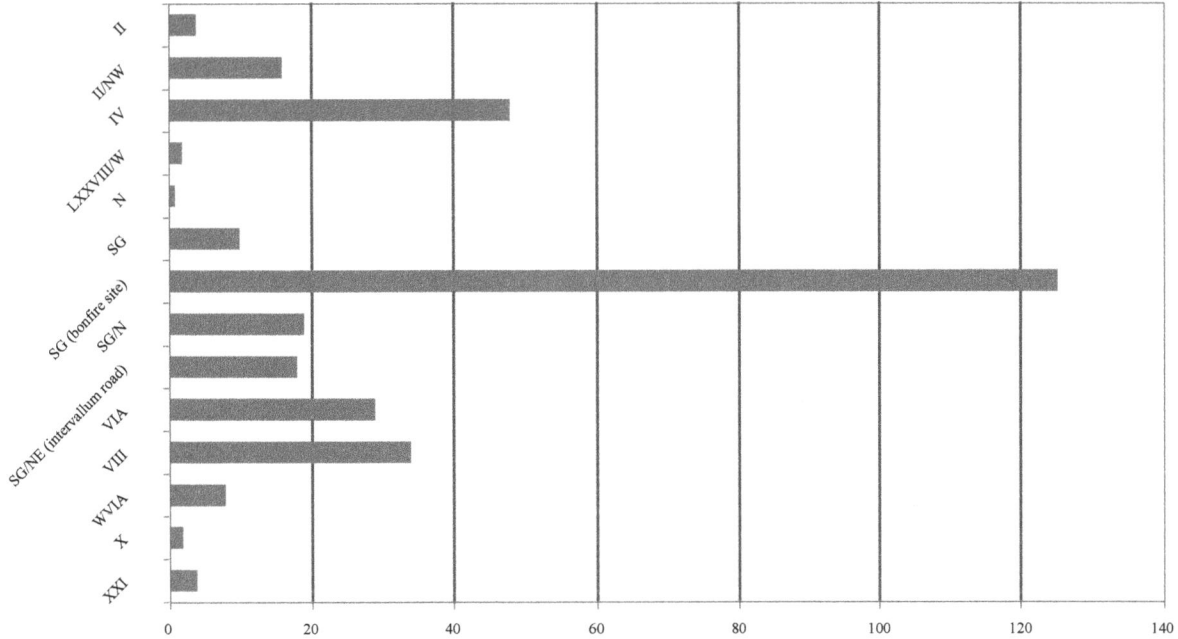

Fig. 3: Transactions by Find Spot, Period III

Equally important is the fact that the surviving evidence suffers from a temporal and spatial bias induced by the archaeological circumstances and the gradual process of excavation: more tablets have been unearthed from the middle periods than from the others, and more thorough excavations have been carried out around the area of the successive *praetoria*, that is, 'commanders' residences.' A quantification and analysis of all of the transactions that can be identified with any certainty in the Vindolanda Tablets makes it possible to illustrate the temporal and spatial biases as in **Fig. 2**.[12]

As **Fig. 2** shows, 'Period III,' the years c. AD 97/100–05, when Flavius Cerialis was prefect, supplies by far the greatest amount of evidence for economic activity at Vindolanda. If we further analyse the transactions of Period III and group them according to their archaeological 'find spots' (cf. **Fig. 3**), we see that a clear majority originates from 'SG (bonfire site),' that is to say, the 'South Gate bonfire site' which lay immediately outside the Period III *praetorium* and was where the archives of Cerialis were burnt prior to his cohort's departure from Vindolanda in AD 105.[13]

To sum up, we would expect the evidence of economic activity attested by the Vindolanda Tablets to be dominated by events in Period III in general and by matters related to the running of the *praetorium* of Flavius Cerialis in particular.

As concerns the temporal bias, it is not of any great

---

[12] This quantitative approach is based on an analysis of *Tab.Vindol.* I–III, the results of which are to be found in a summarised form in the Appendix (the recently published *Tab.Vindol.* IV.i contains altogether too few new findings to alter the results in any way).
[13] R. Birley (ed.), *The Early Wooden Forts: The Excavations of 1973–76 and 1985–89, with Some Additional Details from the Excavations of 1991–93*, Vindolanda Research Reports, New Series I (Hexham, 1994), see map between pp. 60 and 61; this work cited hereafter as *VRR* I.

consequence since the fort of Vindolanda was occupied continually by successive cohorts originating from about the same region on the Rhine frontier.[14] However, it is worth keeping in mind that each cohort had its own established, internal organisation, and that during each individual residency, therefore, a specific community took shape within the walls of the fort while a multi-layered economy emerged around it. The transition-phase which took place when there was a change of garrison would therefore represent a short hiatus in which ties between a cohort and the wider society around the fort were severed and then had to be re-constituted by the new arrivals.

More significantly, the spatial bias has serious implications for the nature of the evidence as the charts above show that the identifiable transactions do not constitute a true representation of the relative importance of different kinds of economic behaviour within the military community. Thus, although quantitative methods can be applied to this collection of data, it is of the utmost importance to consider the biased nature of the evidence and to limit any conclusions accordingly.

The role of the early civilian community that grew up outside the gates of the successive forts also needs to be considered, for although the civilian status of some of the economic agents mentioned in the tablets is certain, it is difficult to distinguish between civilian and military spheres of activity in general. The presence of 'trading camps,' *vici*, outside Roman forts is well attested, however,[15] and the present day Vindolanda site even boasts its own impressive remains of civilian houses in stone from later periods than those considered here.[16]

Although there is hardly any positive evidence, textual or archaeological, for the earliest *vicus* of Vindolanda, circumstantial evidence in the tablets suggests that such a settlement did indeed exist at the time in question: one tablet mentions 'revenues of the fort,' *reditus castelli*, which may indicate a taxable or commercially active civilian presence outside the walls;[17] and another tablet refers to 'oxherds in the woods,' *bubulcaris in silvam*, and swine- and oxherds in general.[18] In addition, an altar stone of unknown date bears a communal inscription by the *vicani vindolandesses*, while yet another stone is dedicated to 'Divine Mercury,' the god of trade—implying resident worshippers of a less war-like and more mercantile cast.[19]

Finally, a comparable military establishment like the fort of *Vindonissa*—in Raetia, occupied *ca.* AD 30–101—boasts similar sources for an adjacent civilian settlement: *vicani vindonissenses* are mentioned in two inscriptions; traders, *negotiatores*, who were also *cives Romani*, crop up in a third inscription; and women, civilian bathhouses and a merchant are attested in two surviving fragments of writing-tablets.[20]

On a more general note, moreover, the Vindolandan evidence can be supplemented and compared with at least four other *corpora* in addition to the *corpus* of tablets from *Vindonissa*:[21] the *ostraca* of Bu Njem, the *ostraca* of *Mons Claudianus*, the *papyri* of *Dura-Europus* and the Carlisle Tablets. At the site of Bu Njem (Latin: *Golas*) in Libya, a frontier garrison in the desert manned by local auxiliaries, a collection of *ostraca* dating from AD 253–59, and mostly written by lowly clerks, have been unearthed.[22] However, an even larger collection of *ostraca* from the early half of the second century AD has been excavated at a Roman fortification in the eastern Egyptian desert guarding the stone quarries of *Mons Claudianus*,[23] while *Dura-Europus*, on the other hand, was an important fortress-town of Greco-Macedonian origin in the middle of the Syrian desert, held by a cohort of Palmyrene archers and legionary detachments, which has yielded a highly interesting archive of *papyri* dealing with military matters in the period AD 205–56.[24] And finally, the Carlisle Tablets share the same origin as the Vindolanda Tablets: they are contemporary writing-tablets from the westernmost part, *Luguvalium*, of the Stanegate Road frontier system.[25]

Having now provided an outline of the aims of this study and its subject matter, the first chapter will examine the historiographical background to the issues which will be considered in subsequent chapters.

---

[14] See map, chapter six, p. 46. For ancient authors on the Batavians, see Tacitus, *Germania*, 29.1; *Historiae*, 4.12; and Caesar, *Bellum Gallicum*, 4.10; and on the Tungrians, see Tacitus, *Germania*, 2.2; A. R. Birley, *Garrison Life*, p. 41, contains a chapter dealing with the two tribes.
[15] Cf. C. R. Whittaker, 'Supplying the Army: Evidence from Vindolanda,' in P. Erdkamp (ed.), *The Roman Army and the Economy* (Amsterdam, 2002), pp. 216–17.
[16] A. R. Birley, *Garrison Life*, p. 55.
[17] *Tab.Vindol.* II.178, l. 1.
[18] *Tab.Vindol.* II.180, l. 9, in particular.
[19] R. G. Collingwood and R. P. Wright (eds), *Roman Inscriptions in Britain* (Oxford, 1965), numbers 1,700 and 1,693, respectively; this work cited hereafter as *RIB* I. See also Bowman, *Life and Letters*, pp. 78–79.
[20] Epigraphy: *vicani Vindonissenses* are mentioned in *CIL* XIII 5,195 (from AD 79) and XIII 5,194; *negotiatores* who are *cives Romani* in XIII 5,221; and *cives Romani* in XIII 11,518. Tablets: *Tab.Vindon.* 44 is addressed to a woman living 'above the bathhouse' and *Tab.Vindon.* 47 to a resident wine merchant.
[21] M. A. Speidel (ed.), *Die römischen Schreibtafeln von Vindonissa* (Brugg, 1996); cited hereafter as *Tab.Vindon.*
[22] R. Marichal (ed.), *Les Ostraca de Bu Njem* (Tripoli, 1992); cited hereafter as *O.Bu.Njem.*
[23] J. Bingen *et al.* (eds.), *Mons Claudianus. Ostraca Graeca et Latina*, vols. I–IV (Cairo, 1992–2009); cited hereafter as *O.Claud.*
[24] C. B. Welles *et al.* (eds.), *The Excavations at Dura-Europus, Final Report V, Part I: The Parchments and Papyri* (New Haven, 1959); cited hereafter as *P.Dura-Europus.*
[25] R. S. O. Tomlin (ed.), 'Roman Manuscripts from Carlisle: The Ink-Written Tablets' in *Britannia*, 29 (1998), 31–84; cited hereafter as *Tab.Luguval.*

Chapter 1
The Ancient Economy: Historiography and Theory

The faint beginnings of the current view on the ancient economy, and the development of a sub-discipline with that particular focus, are rooted in a struggle between German classicists of the 1890s: the so-called 'Bücher-Meyer Controversy.'[1] Basically, this controversy revolved around the scale of the ancient economy: was it primarily based on the individual household and self-sufficiency, or could it be envisaged as commercial, capitalistic and even, in some ways, proto-industrial? Bücher claimed the former, Meyer the latter, and out of this disagreement the primitivist-modernist debate was born.

The adherents of Bücher were proponents of differentiating between ancient society and its modern counterpart. They stressed the specific and unique nature of antiquity whilst downplaying the role of trade and industry for the peoples of Greece and Rome: the defining characteristic of the ancient economy was its fundamental primitivism. On the other hand, the followers of Meyer claimed that the difference was not qualitative, but only quantitative, and that the ancients differed from us only as a result of the technological progress since then—the crucial point was the social and structural similarities between the Ancient World and the Modern one.

Along the lines sketched above, the primitivists envisaged the ancient economy as basically backward, agrarian and therefore also of a limited scope. The modernists, however, considered trade and commercial activity to have played a much larger part in society alongside the workings of the agrarian economy. Furthermore, the level of antagonism between these two schools reached new heights as the controversy entered the battleground of discourse theory: the primitivists contesting the right of the modernists to apply 'modern' terms to social and economic phenomena of antiquity. Hence, the term 'modernising' in ancient history has come to mean drawing a false analogy by describing things using a modern vocabulary. 'Primitivising,' on the other hand, implies that an author is stressing the small scale of the economy and underdeveloped level of commercial activity too forcefully.[2]

In order properly to comprehend this debate, it is necessary to keep in mind that the nineteenth century witnessed a much greater conflict within the discipline of history regarding basic tenets of scientific theory: the opposition between the historicist and positivist schools of thought. Historicism stressed the unique qualitative nature of any period in history and claimed that interpretation was highly dependent on appreciating the specific character of that given period in time. In contrast, positivism posited the qualitative equality of all ages and that such things as fundamental, historical 'laws' or 'concepts' existed. The two theoretical conflicts were not identical, but they were tied in with each other in so far as the primitivist-modernist debate was an inter-disciplinary struggle that branched off from a more generally scientific one.[3]

However, to return to the historiographical survey, the primitivist-modernist debate raged on unabated and with no side getting the upper hand until the publication of the works of M. I. Rostovtzeff, especially his *A Social and Economic History of the Hellenistic World*, which appeared in 1941. In fact, Rostovtzeff stated as early as 1933 that: 'by the Hellenistic period the economy of the ancient world was only quantitatively, not qualitatively, different from that of modern times.'[4] The primitivists, of course, did not agree at all, but nobody could for the time being match the monumental scope of Rostovtzeff's work. Nonetheless, one other author of the 1930s, Johannes Hasebroek, was of great importance because of the influence his writings were to have on a later scholar, Moses Finley.

Hasebroek criticised the modernist approach of Rostovtzeff and his peers, but also suggested modifications to the primitivist model: hitherto, the basic economic unit of antiquity had been considered the single household, but Hasebroek introduced the free, Greek city-state, *polis*, as the new basic frame of reference. He argued that the individual city's paramount concern was the ability to supply grain to its citizens, and that this aspect of the economy was far predominant at the expense of trade. As a consequence, commercial activity was relegated to an inferior level of importance in his model.[5]

A new approach was then introduced in the late 1940s by the economic historian Karl Polanyi. He argued that modern economics are the embodiment of the price-setting market as a culturally instituted process of

---

[1] The main writings of the controversy were republished, still in German, by M. Finley (ed.), *The Bücher-Meyer Controversy* (New York, 1979).
[2] For a brief outline of the whole controversy, see N. Morley, *Theories, Models and Concepts in Ancient History* (New York, 2004), pp. 37–43.
[3] Cf. P. F. Bang, *The Roman Bazaar: A Comparative Study of Trade and Markets in a Tributary Empire* (Cambridge, 2008), pp. 20–21.
[4] M. I. Rostovtzeff, *The Social and Economic History of the Hellenistic World* (Oxford, 1941); and quote from M. I. Rostovtzeff, 'Review of J. Hasebroek, *Griechische Wirtschafts- und Gesellschaftsgeschichte* (Tübingen, 1931),' in *Zeitschrift für die gesamte Staatswissenschaft*, 92 (1933), 333–9.
[5] For Hasebroek's model, see Morley, *Theories, Models and Concepts*, pp. 39–40; and M. Nafissi, *Ancient Athens and Modern Ideology: Value, Theory and Evidence in Historical Sciences* (London, 2005), pp. 219–20.

exchange, and that, as a consequence of this, different societies, both past and present, have had different social institutions which have affected their respective economies in different ways.[6] Hence, market theory could not necessarily be extrapolated back into the past, in just the same way as anthropologists would be hesitant to interpret the exchange of goods between native tribesmen in a capitalist manner. Instead, Polanyi conceived of the human economy as being 'embedded and enmeshed in institutions, economic and non-economic. The inclusion of the non-economic is vital.'[7]

This entailed focusing on redistribution and reciprocity as alternatives to the traditional market-mediated process, as the exchange of goods and services was to be considered embedded in the social dimension of life. The individual economic agent would then be acting not only out of a quest for profit, but also affected and motivated by specific social relations. Accordingly, the validity of traditional, capitalist, economic analysis was undermined, as the mechanism of supply and demand was impaired by a multitude of non-rational concerns. The existence of an independent and autonomous 'economic sphere' of society was questioned, and economic activity was subsumed into the social aspects of daily life, which were highly dependent on the specific culture in question.[8]

Polanyi's approach came to be named 'substantivism' and a theoretical antithesis, 'formalism,' immediately sprang out of the ensuing debate. The formalists claiming that the tenets of modern economics are based on a set of universal principles that have always been common to pre-industrial and modern man alike. Therefore, the ancients did perceive of a 'formal' economic sphere of life (hence the name), and they also knew of and employed the price-setting market.[9]

The substantivist and formalist approaches were not completely mutually exclusive, as is apparent in Polanyi's inclusion of the market as a means of exchange, but they did stress opposite modes of economic behaviour. This was a question about the quality of ancient economic activity: how was economic life, the exchange of values, organised and institutionalised at the most basic level? However, it is vital to keep in mind that the substantivist-formalist debate was of a fundamentally different kind to its primitivist-modernist counterpart: the former concerned the nature or quality of exchange, whereas the latter was about the scale or quantity of economic activity.

Furthermore, the added theoretical dispute over Polanyi's 'substantivist concept' did nothing to help with the still ongoing struggle between basically primitivist or modernist authors of ancient history—if anything, there was now even more room for differing accounts of the same subject. This was nowhere more apparent than with the works of A. H. M. Jones and M. Finley.[10] Both were based on primitivist views, but Jones and Finley had widely different perceptions of the importance to be accorded 'economic embeddedness' in a work on the ancient economy.

In his collected essays, *The Roman Economy: Studies in Ancient Economic and Administrative History* (published after his death in 1973), Jones revealed a remarkably primitivist and formalist view of the ancient economy: the Roman Empire with its huge conquests and extensive infrastructure had created ample scope for trade and industry on a large scale—but neither ever developed beyond the marketing of luxury goods for consumption by the upper class, as might otherwise have been expected. Such price-setting markets regulated by supply and demand as did exist were inhibited by lack of demand due to widespread reliance on the internal economy of the private, self-sufficient, estate and the disruptive effects of a huge, official, command economy.[11]

All in all, Jones continued the primitivist tradition without making room in his model for the new substantivist ideas, and his work can in many ways be considered a primitivist response to Rostovtzeff's overly modernising publications. The theoretical deadlock might well have continued, therefore, had it not been for the appearance in these years of Moses Finley's Sather Lectures, for Finley's basic approach consisted in reaching back to Hasebroek's model of the 1930s and revising it using the theoretical tools developed since then in the substantivist-formalist debate. Thus, he explained the lack of trade inherent in Hasebroek's model by arguing that ancient economic activity was subject to the social relations of Greco-Roman life, and that there was no independent economic sphere because it was, in fact, embedded in society at large.[12]

Although Finley attended seminars held by Polanyi in the late 1940s and early 1950s,[13] he did not acknowledge any explicit debt to him. This can in part be explained by the fact that both Finley and Polanyi in their models drew heavily on Max Weber and his theory about the

---

[6] K. Polanyi, 'The Economy as Instituted Process' in K. Polanyi, C. Arensberg and H. W. Pearson (eds), *Trade and Market in the Early Empires* (1957; Chicago, 1971), pp. 247–50; and W. C. Neale, 'The Market in Theory and History' in K. Polanyi, C. Arensberg and H. W. Pearson (eds), *Trade and Market in the Early Empires* (1957; Chicago, 1971), p. 364.
[7] Polanyi, 'The Economy as Instituted Process,' pp. 249–50.
[8] K. Polanyi, *The Great Transformation* (1944; New York, 1978), p. 46; and K. Polanyi, 'Aristotle Discovers the Economy', in K. Polanyi, C. Arensberg and H. W. Pearson (eds), *Trade and Market in the Early Empires* (1957; Chicago, 1971), p. 71.
[9] Morley, *Theories, Models and Concepts*, p. 43.
[10] Jones's essays on economic history are collected in his *The Roman Economy. Studies in Ancient Economic and Administrative History*, ed. P. A. Brunt (Oxford, 1974), whilst Finley's views are usefully pulled in his *The Ancient Economy*, Sather Lectures (London, 1973), recently reprinted in an expanded edition with a foreword by I. Morris (Berkeley and Los Angeles, 1999).
[11] Jones, *The Roman Economy*, p. 129.
[12] For Finley's use of this model, see Nafissi, *Ancient Athens and Modern Ideology*, p. 222.
[13] Bang, *The Roman Bazaar*, pp. 23–24.

ascendancy of class over status in nineteenth-century Western Europe, which implied that the role of the market had been widely different in earlier societies.[14]

However, two things that are not necessarily obvious are important to point out when it comes to Finley's ideas: firstly, that his model was based on a combination of primitivism and substantivism (even though he did not himself apply these terms), and secondly, that his grand vision tended towards being more of a negative description than a positive model; that is, Finley went to great lengths to tell his reader how the ancient economy was *not* constituted, but he revealed disproportionately little about how it actually worked. However, the basic—and most historiographically important—tenet of his model was as follows:

> What if a society was not organised for the satisfaction of its material wants by 'an enormous conglomeration of interdependent markets?' It would then not be possible to discover or formulate laws of economic behaviour, without which a concept of 'the economy' is unlikely to develop.[15]

This was based on the assumption that the ancient Greco-Roman social élites were much more concerned with their relative status in society than with employing their assets to obtain a profit. On the contrary, they fostered an ideology which considered the ownership of landed estates the prime source of social and political status, and therefore commercial activity, manufacture and 'industry' were relegated to people outside the upper class and further down in the social hierarchy of status.[16]

In addition, Finley deployed a primitivist argument against any large-scale trading activity: due to an inadequate development of transport technology it was, quite simply, almost impossible to make a profit out of long-distance trading. To be sure, there was some trade which was made possible by sea transport, but it was hampered by an extensive, empire-wide economy of self-sufficiency, which itself was the product of the high transport expenses.[17] Combining these two arguments, Finley basically constructed a traditional primitivist account of the ancient economy, but his masterstroke was the creation of a historical work successfully incorporating substantivist thought and thereby portraying an embedded economy.

Ever since it was first published, *The Ancient Economy* has been subjected to a wide variety of criticism: 'new cultural historians' and 'undersocialisation critics' claimed that it was too materialist; 'empiricists' argued that the model did not account sufficiently for the details and particulars of antiquity; 'oversocialisation' critics claimed that Finley put too much weight on the importance and consequences of social relationships; and lastly, Finley was accused of plain primitivism.[18] The thing is, though, that until recently nobody was able to supply a better social and economic framework than the one provided by Finley's model. For more than twenty years Keith Hopkins, himself a pupil of Finley and arguably the most famous historian of the ancient economy in the generation after Finley, refined a fascinating 'core-periphery' model of the economy of the Roman Empire, but his basic assumption as to society in general was that 'the Finley model... is by far the best model available.'[19] Nonetheless, modernist views still persist, and some commentators have assumed that the old impasse will continue much as before.[20]

However, in light of the many years spent in a theoretical stalemate and considering the diverse interpretations of Finley's work, some pioneering historians of antiquity have chosen to turn away from this never-ending theoretical struggle and have tried to shape a new way of researching and writing ancient economic history. The new approach generally acknowledges that the ancient economy displayed features of all four different primitivist-modernist and formalist-substantivist models —sometimes at once, sometimes at different places and at different times. Hence, historians must try to shed their basic assumptions as to the scale and nature of the subject studied (acknowledging at the same time that absolute objectivity is neither possible nor desired), and instead try to let the evidence and their research guide them. Accordingly, the only tenet common to all advocates of the new approach is that we must acknowledge the complexity of the ancient economy.[21]

The problem is, though, that the more tentative our conclusions become, the more restricted they become as well, and the less we base our models on assumptions *in lieu* of non-existing ancient evidence, the less they tend to explain and illustrate. However, if that is the

---

[14] I. Morris, 'Foreword,' in M. Finley, *The Ancient Economy. Updated with a New Foreword by Ian Morris* (1973; Berkeley and Los Angeles, 1999), pp. xvii and xvi, respectively.
[15] Finley, *The Ancient Economy*, p. 22.
[16] Finley, *The Ancient Economy*: for the economic aspects of landownership, pp. 108-110; for the ideological pp. 96–7, 111, 116–17, 121–22, 147, 188; and for trade and industry's marginalisation to socially inferior groups, pp. 60, 75–6, 140, 144–45.
[17] Finley, *The Ancient Economy*, pp. 126–28 and 138, respectively.
[18] Morris, 'Foreword,' pp. xxiv-xxix.
[19] The quote is from K. Hopkins, 'Introduction' in P. Garnsey, K. Hopkins and C. R. Whittaker (eds), *Trade in the Ancient Economy* (London, 1983), p. xiv; and the first version of the model was K. Hopkins, 'Taxes and Trade in the Roman Empire (200 BC–AD 400),' in *Journal of Roman Studies*, 70 (1980), 101–125.
[20] For a well-developed modernist model, see for instance W. V. Harris, 'Between Archaic and Modern: Some Current Problems in the History of the Roman Economy' in W. V. Harris (ed.), *The Inscribed Economy: Production and Distribution in the Roman Empire in the Light of Instrumentum Domesticum. The Proceedings of a Conference Held at the American Academy in Rome on 10–11th January, 1992* (Ann Arbor, MN; 1993), pp. 11–29.
[21] Two different publications displaying similar approaches would be: W. Scheidel and S. von Reden (eds), *The Ancient Economy* (Edinburgh, 2002); and Z. Archibald, J. K. Davies, V. Gabrielsen and G. J. Oliver (eds), *Hellenistic Economies* (London and New York, 2001). A discussion of new ways to avoid old theoretical pitfalls is provided in J. K. Davies, 'Linear and Nonlinear Flow Models for Ancient Economies' in J. G. Manning and I. Morris (eds), *The Ancient Economy. Evidence and Models* (Stanford, 2005), pp. 127–156.

consequence, so be it. Less explanatory models are far superior to models based on unsubstantiated notions that the ancient economy was 'small' or 'large,' 'embedded' or 'proto-industrial.' Moreover, these new complex models need not be less informative at all, if they are based on meticulous studies of the time and place which they are constructed to help explain.

Hopefully, this chapter has managed to outline and elucidate the historiography of the ancient economy and some of the theoretical controversies pertaining to it. Specifically, that after more than a century's debate there is still no agreement as to the scale of ancient economic activity or even its very nature. Therefore, throughout this study, the latest 'complex view' will be the approach adopted as different aspects of the economic activity at Vindolanda will be interpreted in different ways—without adhering to one overall model or theory. In this way, the challenge is not to reduce the complexity of the sources, but the opposite: to account for their ambiguity and contradictory nature.

More specifically, the Vindolanda Tablets will be used to shed light on the overarching questions of quality and quantity in the ancient economy. For example, a comparative analysis of a number of traders' accounts, business letters and related texts can tell us how extensive the use of ready cash was in a frontier zone; which commodities travelled and who bought them; what kind of transactions took place; how big the market for private consumption was and what role private entrepreneurs played in the supply of the Roman army. These are all questions which are intimately related to debates concerning the nature and scale of economic activity in a frontier zone—and, exercising due caution, we might even become wiser about the ancient economy in general.

Furthermore, the questions raised above reflect only on what we can learn from the role of the market in the Vindolandan military community: for a comprehensive understanding of the economic activity as a whole, it is also necessary to delve into the matter of state redistribution as illuminated by official accounts of grain disbursements, weapon supply, lists of soldiers on duty in workshops, all sorts of minor and major repairs, transport, and so on—and the evidence is there, neatly written on small wooden tablets.

In fact, having just sketched the uses of the Vindolanda Tablets for research into the nature of market activity and state redistribution, one can even go as far as trying to uncover economic relations based on reciprocity, that is to say, embedded in the social institutions of this particular kind of military society: the economic role of the prefect, lower officers, religious practices and more general, cultural phenomena. All the topics and issues mentioned here relate directly to the theoretical controversies discussed above, and the value and importance of this new, Vindolandan data for the study of the ancient economy should therefore be evident.

Chapter 2
The Economy of Roman Britain: Evidence and Historiography

The purpose of the present chapter is to narrow the focus from the ancient economy as a whole to the time and place specific to this study. By providing a brief outline of the economy of Roman Britain, of the available traditional evidence and of the important secondary works on the topic, a basis will be provided for the interpretation of all that is new, significant and controversial in the Vindolanda Tablets.

However, it needs to be stressed at the outset that this chapter is not about Hadrian's Wall and its garrison's influence on the economy of the northern frontier—for the Wall and the absolute majority of the Vindolanda Tablets are not contemporary, as less than five per cent of the total amount of transactions attested by the tablets date from Period V, that is the years c. AD 120–28.[1] In fact, the construction of Hadrian's Wall only began in AD 122 and parts of it were not finished until AD 128 at the earliest.[2] Hence, as nearly all of the evidence of economic activities attested by the tablets predate both the Wall itself and any conception of such a monumental frontier system, it would be anachronistic and fraught with problems to compare the early Flavian and Trajanic frontiers with the institutionalised supply system of one of the most elaborate and long-lived frontiers of the Western Empire.

Rather, the evidence of the Vindolanda Tablets needs to be seen in the context of the economy which supported the Flavian and Trajanic frontier systems. These were based on defence in depth, settled loosely on the Tyne-Solway line and the east-west military road with its seven forts (constructed by Agricola) which has became known as the Stanegate Road. Any comparisons between the Stanegate Road and Hadrian's Wall are made difficult by our lack of knowledge about the former, but it is quite certain that the construction of the Wall resulted in a concentration of garrison forces (sixteen forts on the Wall alone and more than 10,000 auxiliaries) on a hitherto unprecedented scale which must have caused the supply system to undergo substantial readjustment or even complete reestablishment.[3]

As a consequence, rather than extrapolating research done on the supply of the Hadrian's Wall garrison throughout nearly three centuries of occupation to the supply situation of the Stanegate frontier, this chapter will endeavour to account for the historiography of the early economy of the province as a whole, especially as it relates to highland society and the economic role and influence of the army. Moreover, the views of recent authors dealing directly with the subject of army supply attested by the Vindolanda Tablets will be discussed in chapter six, when the results of our investigations of the evidence in chapters three, four and five are assessed and compared with the present state of research.

The traditional evidence
In spite of the paucity of ancient literary evidence for Roman Britain, there is a small *corpus* of ancient texts all pertaining to the history of the province;[4] the two authors most relevant to a study of the early economy of Roman Britain being, in chronological order, Strabo and Tacitus. Strabo (born *ca*. 64 BC; died sometime after AD 21), Greek historian and geographer, is perhaps the most frequently quoted author of antiquity in historical works on the subject. In his *Geographica*, published in the reign of Tiberius (emperor AD 14–37), he briefly described the geography of the isle of Britain before mentioning its exports and later on alluding to the heavy duties paid on cross-Channel trade.[5] His list of commodities produced and traded is one of the best pieces of evidence available for economic activity in pre-Roman and, by extension, early Roman Britain.

The more substantial of the two narratives, however, is the work *Agricola*, written by the Roman senator Cornelius Tacitus (born *ca*. AD 56; died sometime after AD 118) in honour of his father-in-law, Julius Agricola, governor of the province of Roman Britain AD 77–83. The account was published in AD 98 and is a description of Agricola's northern campaigns that won him control, even if only very short-lived, over the northern tribes of highland Scotland. It was Agricola's victories that provided the basis of what was to develop into the northern frontier, and the events related are almost contemporaneous with some of the earliest Vindolanda Tablets.

An alternative source of written testimony is that provided by epigraphy: a very sizeable *corpus* of inscriptions has been discovered in Britain and published for wider study. For editorial reasons the epigraphical evidence has been divided into two separate volumes: the older '*Inscriptions on Stone*' and a more recent publication (consisting of a series of fascicules) dealing with inscriptions from *instrumentum domesticum*.[6]

---

[1] See **Fig. 2**, p. 3, and Appendix.
[2] Frere, *Britannia*, p. 117.
[3] Regarding the development of the Stanegate frontier, see Frere, *Britannia*, pp. 106–9, 117–18; and D. Shotter, *Roman Britain*, 2nd edn (London, 2004), pp. 36–37.
[4] H. Petrie and J. Sharpe (eds), *Monumenta Historica Britannica* (London, 1848); and of more recent date and more easily accessible: Mann and Penman (eds), *Literary Sources for Roman Britain* (London, 1996).
[5] Strabo, *Geographica*, 4.5.2 (199)–4.5.3 (200).
[6] *RIB* I; and S.S. Frere (ed.), *The Roman Inscriptions of Britain* (Stroud, 1995); the latter conveniently referred to as *RIB* II.

However, the most abundant body of evidence for Roman Britain is that constituted by the archaeological record: formal excavations have been going on for more than two centuries, and in the twentieth century as a whole so many significant finds were made, excavated and published that any book on the subject was beginning to be outdated within a decade or so. Accordingly, the major works written in the last century have all been heavily reliant on the interpretation of material remains for all of those aspects of economy and society not dealt with by the meagre literary sources.

The historiography of the early economy
Arguably the most influential history of Roman Britain produced in the twentieth century was that of R. G. Collingwood, historian and archaeologist, in 1936.[7] It pre-dated any wider and more critical discussion of the capitalist notion of the 'economy,' and, as a consequence, Collingwood employed words such as 'concentrated capitalistic production and free individualistic industry' freely.[8]

Collingwood's view on the economic development of the province was that after the Claudian invasion of AD 43 the import of luxury goods rose to enormous proportions as the native élite sought to accommodate the new rulers by assimilating the style and material culture of the conquerors. Any increase in agricultural production was consumed within the province itself by the army and the Roman administration. Native industries were developed by craftsmen producing second-class quality goods, and, in consequence, there was much less import in the Hadrianic period (AD 117–38); moreover, as the province had to rely more and more on its own resources, there was increasing urban and rural prosperity.[9]

As regards the internal infrastructure and economic activity, the Roman roads were excellent for official traffic, but they were not of much use for local traffic, as they were laid out to service political centres not population centres.[10] Subsequently, Collingwood then went on to describe, in one paragraph, how internal trade was facilitated by using town *fora*, country markets and itinerant hawkers.[11]

In keeping with his somewhat primitivist view of the economy, he accounted for urban and rural life by informing his reader that the towns of Roman Britain were parasitic and essentially a thing of luxury, but that they had important political and cultural functions;[12] and that the countryside, where the great majority of the population was occupied in agriculture, encompassed two different economic systems: one consisting of the villas of the Romanised, native élite and one of British villages inhabited by free property-owners or dependents of either the villa-owners or imperial estates. The villas were predominantly the country-houses and farms of the rich, but in some rare cases villas developed into 'factories,' and many villages were 'industrial,' although most were agricultural.[13]

This description of Romano-British society was applicable only to the lowland zone with its cities and villas, but as regards the societies of the highland zone, what little data there was just led Collingwood to conclude that there was evidence of a dense and increasing population under Roman rule, and that there was a lot of trade across the northern frontier to Scotland.[14]

However, although the general picture is still roughly the same, an important new contribution appeared just twenty years later, in 1955, when I. A. Richmond expanded and revised some of Collingwood's conclusions. Firstly, Richmond claimed that 'the normal Roman villa was not a liability ... but a profit-making farm' (which was not necessarily implied in Collingwood's 'country-house' model);[15] secondly, he asserted that 'the thick clusters of huts and storage-pits which made up the native farm used regularly to be interpreted as a village' and that therefore, in complete contradiction with Collingwood, 'the broad distinction is to be drawn no longer between villas and villages, but between landowners and their tenants or their neighbour small-holders;'[16] and thirdly, Richmond argued that 'if in southern Britain there is some evidence of expansion of pastoralism at the expense of agriculture, in northern Britain the process was probably reversed. There is little evidence for agriculture on any scale but the smallest in the north in pre-Roman days.'[17]

Only three years later, in 1958, another book was published by A. L. F. Rivet which, although bearing the slightly different title *Town and Country in Roman Britain*, was very much like the previous general histories. Rivet pointed to the substantial number of Roman towns which have enjoyed continued occupation ever since their founding almost 2000 years ago and concluded that 'the exploitation of Britain's agricultural wealth in Roman times was neither so limited nor so primitive as we sometimes tend to assume. The pattern is strikingly modern.'[18]

---

[7] R. G. Collingwood and J. N. L. Myres, *Roman Britain and the English Settlements* (Oxford, 1936).
[8] Collingwood, *Roman Britain*, p. 237.
[9] Collingwood, *Roman Britain*, pp. 226–27.
[10] Collingwood, *Roman Britain*, p. 240.
[11] Collingwood, *Roman Britain*, p. 244.
[12] Collingwood, *Roman Britain*, pp. 198–99.
[13] Collingwood, *Roman Britain*, pp. 208–24.
[14] Collingwood, *Roman Britain*, pp. 176–77, 181 and 245, respectively.
[15] I. A. Richmond, *Roman Britain* (Harmondsworth, Middlesex; 1955) p. 109.
[16] Richmond, *Roman Britain*, pp. 125–6.
[17] Richmond, *Roman Britain*, p. 132.
[18] A. L. F. Rivet, *Town and Country in Roman Britain* (London, 1964), p. 76.

This emphasis on the significance of Roman towns was important, because Rivet went on to argue for a special connection between towns and villas, that is to say between town and countryside: 'Provided, therefore, that we bear in mind the agricultural undertones, we may, for our own purposes, restrict the use of "villa" somewhat and lay rather more stress on the degree of civilisation of the occupant,'[19] which led him to conclude that in the first and second centuries AD, the process of Romanisation in Britain was 'centripetal' (inwardly focused on the urban sphere of society) unlike in Italy where it was held to be 'centrifugal' (isolationist).[20]

As regards Rivet's views on the economy and society of the highland zones, his words basically echoed those of Richmond: the inhabitants were peasants and herdsmen 'whose way of life was little affected by the conquest.'[21] However, as concerns the internal trade of the province he had one last significant point to add, namely that 'as trade developed and political control became centralised ... the markets tended to become permanently located in the towns which formed the natural commercial centres'. Rivet stressed this point because 'this connection between town and country is important throughout the Roman occupation. In the early stages it largely determined which of the farms became Romanised...'[22] Rivet's work was important simply because it emphasised the close connection and mutual interdependence of town and country in a new and more forceful way.

Whereas the subject matter of the works of Richmond and Rivet had been firmly determined by the mainly archaeological perspectives of these authors, a new and more traditional history of Roman Britain, focused more on chronology than on types of material remains, was published by S. S. Frere in 1967.

Frere was in agreement with Rivet as regards a general move away from the notion of the 'parasitical' city of antiquity and described the influence of town on countryside as follows:

> From the towns their products, and the classical influence which they represented, reached out to the wealthy villa-owners in the surrounding districts, while the more humdrum products of trade and industry penetrated through the periodic markets to the poorest peasants of the deepest countryside.[23]

But while Frere's view on the social organisation of the countryside was very traditional, he did reintroduce the idea of the 'peasant village' which had otherwise been ousted from Collingwood's model by Richmond.[24] At the same time, he contradicted one of the other basic tenets of Collingwood's model by stating that 'a striking fact about trade and industry in Roman Britain is the ease with which the problems of transport were overcome. Wherever manufactured or produced, goods were easily distributed throughout the province.'[25]

However, the main contribution of Frere's work to the study of economy and society in Roman Britain lay in his more thorough approach to the influence and role of the army and northern garrison on the economy: firstly, the army itself established industries to satisfy its own needs for tiles, pottery, metal-working, hides and so on;[26] and secondly, 'its food-requirements stimulated cereal production in the south and introduced it for the first time to some northern regions,' while at the same time 'its wealth was a standing attraction to merchants.'[27]

An altogether new approach was adopted by J. Wacher in his 1978 publication on Roman Britain, which had as its main focus the population of the province, and in that sense it was neither a classical work of archaeology nor history.[28] All the same, Wacher still covered many of the traditional key topics of the subject, and it can be mentioned in passing that he underlined the importance of towns of differing sizes on trade, and that he asserted that the production of cash crops was facilitated by urban development, roads and currency, while the army made only a 'token payment' for its compulsory share of the harvest.[29]

The most significant consequence of Wacher's focus on the population as a whole was, however, that he did not limit himself to a perfunctory description of the highland communities as being dominantly pastoral with hints of mixed farming here and there—he actually accorded the highland zone a new prominence in accordance with the fact that it constituted more than half the geographical area of the province. Not that Wacher disputed that the highland societies of the South West, Wales, Pennines, Lake District and Scotland were not basically pastoral economies, but after considering the settlement patterns of the different regions in some detail, he argued that 'if the villa is taken to describe the basic agricultural "unit" of the lowland zone, so do these farms ["rounds"] act in the highland areas.'[30] The argument is that highland farms based on a mixed arable and primarily pastoral system were the social and economic counterparts of the

---

[19] Rivet, *Town and Country*, p. 104.
[20] Rivet, *Town and Country*, pp. 104–5.
[21] Rivet, *Town and Country*, p. 117.
[22] Rivet, *Town and Country*, p. 126.
[23] Frere, *Britannia*, p. 254.
[24] Frere, *Britannia*, p. 257.
[25] Frere, *Britannia*, p. 291.
[26] Frere, *Britannia*, pp. 215–16.
[27] Frere, *Britannia*, pp. 217, 260, 265, 281.
[28] J. Wacher, *Roman Britain* (London, 1978).
[29] Wacher, *Roman Britain*, pp. 84, 88, 92, on towns and trade; pp. 106–7, on grain production.
[30] Wacher, *Roman Britain*, p. 139.

Romanised villas, but that they maintained a native way of life due to a 'combination of conservatism and lack of urban markets and influence.'[31]

By 1981 Collingwood's volume on the history of Roman Britain in the old 'Oxford-History-of-England' series had become, as we have seen, outdated on some points, and a new volume by P. Salway was published to replace it. Salway introduced a new and more outspoken theoretical approach which had been sorely needed since the publication of Finley's *The Ancient Economy* in 1973. The historiography of the economy of Roman Britain had never been rife with explicit theoretical assertions, and in answer to the overall model of a primitive, socially embedded economy of the Roman Empire claimed by Finley, Salway chose to argue simply that ancient economic theory could not be properly applied due to lack of evidence and that it tended to simplify phenomena which exhibited many different traits.[32]

Salway provided a comprehensive and combined description of economy and society: the new political and economic opportunities offered by the Roman occupation led to the economic development of towns and countryside and their symbiosis;[33] in the process, the province saw manufacture, industry and commerce on a considerable scale and with the villa as the most important productive system in the countryside.[34]

According to Salway, however, there were two different spheres of economic activity, for on the one hand there was the private sector of the buying public with free play of market forces, while on the other hand, and in marked contrast to this, there were the requirements of the army and government services for which official arrangements existed.[35] The agricultural economy was, however, the basis of both of these dimensions of society, private and public, and whereas the army was supplied by its local highland hinterland, urban areas were supplied by produce from their surrounding villas—the essential Roman factor being the landed estate, existing in a world with a money economy, urban markets and the availability of organised transport.[36]

A different interpretation of many details is to be found in the work of M. Millett. In his book from 1990, Millett conducted a very thorough study of the aspects of economy and society which we have been tracing from the 1930s to the turn of the last century, and in so doing he brought the pattern of historiographical development since Collingwood to an admirable conclusion.[37]

First of all, Millett asserted that although the early villas of Roman Britain should be seen as a result of the Romanisation of the native élite, there is no reason to interpret them automatically as anything but evidence of expenditure and not production.[38] Secondly, he compared the evidence for agricultural activity in Late Pre-Roman Iron Age Celtic Britain with what came after, and he concluded that there was a lack of fundamental agricultural change associated with the Roman invasion, and that accordingly, many of the native farmsteads continued in the old tradition alongside the new villas.[39] Thirdly, Millett suggested that since finds of artefacts reveal a rapid phase of percolation of Roman objects on native sites very soon after the conquest, the goods might have been arriving through existing social networks. This would imply that local economies were themselves integrated into a single, overall socio-economic network which defies the idea of purely subsistence-based farming, and a similar pattern seems to have occurred in areas in the north and west of the province.[40]

As regards the nature of highland society, Millett repeated the statements of his predecessors that there are indicators of mixed arable and pastoral economies in both lowland and highland zones, and that there is 'sound evidence' for a major phase of general agricultural intensification in the last centuries before the Roman Conquest.[41] This would mean that the Roman army, employing a 'logic of necessity,' would have drawn as many of its supplies as possible from local areas, and that the burden of food supply could have been borne by the native agrarian societies.[42]

However, Millett also gave a new explanation for the seeming lack of Romanisation in the north of the province, which he accounted for by arguing that in Scotland, Rome had reached the limit of the type of social organisation which it was possible to incorporate, and, even more importantly, that in areas with a heavy military presence the army actively undermined the emergence of civil authority amongst the native, tribal élites. Therefore, through either warfare or continued military occupation, the Roman presence was socially disruptive.[43]

Concluding remarks on the economy of early Roman Britain
The reason why the historiography of economy and society in early Roman Britain has been dealt with in this way is that this is the historiographical background against which the significance of the Vindolanda Tablets needs to be measured. The unique testimony of the

---

[31] Wacher, *Roman Britain*, p. 135.
[32] P. Salway, *Roman Britain* (Oxford and New York, 1981), pp. 615–18.
[33] Salway, *Roman Britain*, pp. 235–38.
[34] Salway, *Roman Britain*, pp. 625–29.
[35] Salway, *Roman Britain*, p. 650.
[36] Salway, *Roman Britain*, pp. 619–25.
[37] M. Millett, *The Romanization of Britain: An Essay in Archaeological Interpretation* (Cambridge, 1990).
[38] Millett, *The Romanization of Britain*, p. 94.
[39] Millett, *The Romanization of Britain*, pp. 97–98.
[40] Millett, *The Romanization of Britain*, pp. 98–99.
[41] Millett, *The Romanization of Britain*, pp. 10–11.
[42] Millett, *The Romanization of Britain*, pp. 56–57.
[43] Millett, *The Romanization of Britain*, pp. 100–01.

writing-tablets can be used to assess the strengths and weaknesses of the proposed models of the economy and society of Roman Britain, old as new.

If one was to summarise briefly the topics on which there seems to be a tentative consensus, and which have a bearing on the study of economic activity at Vindolanda, it would look as follows: firstly, villas were a cultural phenomenon implying Romanisation, which begs the question why their highland counterparts failed to develop similarly; second, both lowland and highland societies practised mixed arable and pastoral farming, and there is agreement on a steady intensification of farming in the period; third, urban development, the Romanisation of society entailing villas, cash economy, markets and roads, and the expansion of commercial and 'industrial' activity to a level where trade permeated most of the province, speaks of a highly evolved economic system, which began to develop immediately after the conquest, although it did not quite blossom for some time yet to come; and lastly, the Roman army played an economic role through its own 'industrial activity' and by stimulating native producers to intensify both agriculture and manufacturing, albeit mainly in its immediate highland hinterland.

Issues which have a direct bearing on these four points will be discussed in the following three chapters on market activity, redistribution and reciprocity, and the aggregate amount of information which the Vindolanda Tablets yield on these subjects will be summarised in chapter six.

Chapter 3
Market Activity: Traders and Entrepreneurs

A short introduction to the market in theory and practice
In modern English the term 'market' has become somewhat ambiguous, and it would therefore seem prudent to begin this chapter with a concise, utilitarian definition of this word which is frequently used, but less often considered in any great detail.

As an economic concept, the market can be defined as a price-finding mechanism where these prices are decided by a dialogue between mutually opposite forces of supply and demand. The term 'mechanism' refers to the presumption that if either of these two, so-called, market forces of supply and demand change, then it will have an instant effect on its counterpart, and as a consequence prices will be immediately adjusted to suit the new conditions of the market. Hence, the market as a purely theoretical construction is a simple, yet hugely powerful little model of economic activity.[1]

However, it is also a concept to be treated with the utmost caution when it is not applied to the specific phenomenon it was developed to explain: the modern, capitalist, free market. The argument being that pre-industrial societies did not necessarily institutionalise their exchange of goods in accordance with the rules of market theory. Alternative ways of allowing for a smooth exchange of goods have always existed, so it is necessary to consider the nature of any transaction thoroughly before arguing whether it is a case of redistribution, reciprocity or (market) trade.

How, then, are we to perceive of 'trade as market activity?' First of all, by banishing any belief in the mutual exclusivity of social and economic spheres of activity: it is not a question of either formal economic behaviour or completely socially and culturally determined practices, but about their interaction. When money circulates between private individuals it will affect their social relationships by providing a new extra-social frame of reference and vice versa. Furthermore:

> If money gives rise to private transactions between individuals who may profit or lose thereby—transactions which are not regulated in advance by an unchangeable ritual and in which prices are not rigidly fixed—then it is inseparable from certain forms of market...[2]

Only very rarely, or never, will this be the perfect market of modern economists, but it will still be a market in the basic sense of the word.

Enquiries into the importance of the market as a means of exchange have a very direct bearing on the historiography and theory of the ancient economy: reviewing the arguments of Finley, as being representative of a primitivist point of view, the basic tenet is that the ancients 'did not combine these particular [economic] activities conceptually into a unit, "a differentiated sub-system of society",' in other words that there was no awareness of an economic system comprised of an 'enormous conglomeration of interdependent markets,' and that 'there is a fundamental question of method. The economic language and concepts we are all familiar with, the models we employ, tend to draw us into a false account.'[3] Secondly, Finley tells us that all the textual evidence 'confirms' the low status of professional traders and manufacturers, and accordingly 'an investment model in antiquity would give considerable weight to this factor of status.'[4]

Moreover, when it comes down to the trade of landowners, large and small, a system is described where peasant farming was basically subsistence farming—that is, unless 'there were circumstances which may have encouraged peasants, especially those nearer the upper limit of family holdings, to turn to cash crops' (for instance, the nearby presence of a military establishment like Vindolanda); as regards the large landowners, 'they had a "peasant-like" passion for self-sufficiency on their estates,' and 'lacking the techniques by which to calculate and then to choose among the various options, and relishing independence from the market as buyers, from reliance on others for their own necessities, the landowners of antiquity operated by tradition, habit and rule-of-thumb.'[5]

In short, the market was not the preferred means of exchange, and we cannot even talk of an ancient market economy because the ancients themselves were simply not aware of the institution of the market. Those who did trade in anything other than farm produce were politically stigmatised, and those who grew crops were either only marginally concerned with trade or did not have the material or conceptual means to engage in commercial activity in a significant way.

Modernists, on the other hand, have claimed, to differing degrees, that the ancient economy was more or less proto-industrial; that trade and commerce was indeed of consequence; that there was ample room for entrepreneurial activity; and, as a consequence of this and in keeping with formalist arguments, that the Romans did perceive and make use of the role of the market and can

---

[1] See, for instance, Neale, 'The Market in Theory and History,' pp. 357–72; which, although old, is a comprehensive introduction to the theory of the classic, capitalist market.
[2] J. Andreau, *Banking and Business in the Roman World* (Cambridge, 1999), p. 1.
[3] Finley, *The Ancient Economy*, p. 21–23.
[4] Finley, *The Ancient Economy*, p. 59–60.
[5] Finley, *The Ancient Economy*, p. 107 and p. 110.

be considered economic agents in a modern sense.

One such proponent of a modernist and formalist view of the ancient economy is William Harris, who argues that the aggregate demand for basic necessities of life exerted by the big Roman cities on the shores of the Mediterranean would have been enough to create a market economy. The argument being that the demand created by large urban populations, which could not possibly support themselves with food, wine, oil, ceramics and the like, encouraged long-distance trade by stimulating rural areas with access to the sea to produce and distribute wares and commodities on an economically significant scale.[6] The same supply and demand argument, just from a basically primitivist point of view, is used by Hopkins in his model of the Roman economy: the city of Rome's inflow of taxes and rents from the provinces was balanced and counteracted by expenditure on vital imports from these very same provincial areas.[7]

In the following, a variety of tablets providing evidence for the importance of market-mediated exchange at Vindolanda will be analysed and interpreted as regards the different kinds of economic activities they reveal. More specifically, we will be looking for transactions which seem to be determined not by political or social factors, but by the individual economic agent's quest for a profit and use of the market. In so doing, it will be necessary to enquire into the status and motivations of agents: are they acting as civilians or soldiers, in private or official capacities, and what does the purposes of the transactions seem to be? Which goods were traded, between whom and how? This implies the need to examine the size and kinds of commodity markets, the private or institutionalised nature of sellers and buyers, and whether exchange was facilitated by cash, barter or the extension of credit.

Three case studies[8]
In this and the following two chapters, the interpretations and analyses of the relevant sources will be divided into two parts: three longer case studies of tablets selected from a larger *corpus*, followed by an account of the conclusions inferable from that larger *corpus* of tablets relevant to each chapter. The entire amount of transactions which can be ascribed to each kind of economic activity can be surveyed in the Appendix.

Tab.Vindol. II.**343**, in translation:

> Octavius to his brother Candidus, greetings. The hundred pounds of sinew from Marinus—I will settle up. From the time when you wrote about this matter, he has not even mentioned it to me. I have several times written to you that I have bought about five thousand *modii* of ears of grain, on account of which I need cash. Unless you send me some cash, at least five hundred *denarii*, the result will be that I shall lose what I have laid out as a deposit, about three hundred *denarii*, and I shall be embarrassed. So, I ask you, send me some cash as soon as possible. The hides which you write are at *Cataractonium*—write that they be given to me and the wagon about which you write. And write to me what is with that wagon. I would have already been to collect them except that I did not care to injure the animals while the roads are bad. See with Tertius about the 8½ *denarii* which he received from Fatalis. He has not credited them to my account. Know that I have completed the 170 hides and I have 119 *modii* of threshed *bracis*. Make sure that you send me cash so that I may have ears of grain on the threshing-floor. Moreover, I have already finished threshing all that I had. A messmate of our friend Frontius has been here. He was wanting me to allocate (?) him hides and that being so, was ready to give cash. I told him I would give him the hides by 1st March. He decided that he would come on 13th January. He did not turn up nor did he take any trouble to obtain them since he had hides. If he had given the cash, I would have given him them. I hear that Frontinius Iulius has for sale at a high price for leather-working the things which he bought here for five *denarii* apiece. Greet Spectatus and ... and Firmus. I have received letters from Gleuco. Farewell.
>
> (Back) (Deliver) at Vindolanda.[9]

The above letter, in its fully preserved state and with its complete and coherent narrative, is the longest and, arguably, best single piece of evidence for economic activity among all of the tablets unearthed. It was written by a certain Octavius, whose identity and whereabouts are otherwise unknown, to Candidus at Vindolanda. Candidus was, according to the editors, a rather common *cognomen* which crops up in several tablets,[10] but interestingly the name appears in tablets **180** (an account of wheat distribution) and **181** (an account of debts paid and sums owed) which were found close to this letter.

However, we might be able to infer more about the identity of the recipient of the letter, for the tablet was found in 'the rooms at the end of the barracks building,'[11] and according to the standard layout of Roman military establishments this would be where the centurion should be living. Furthermore, it was found among a group of discarded tablets together with tablet **180** where not only the name of Candidus is to be found, but also those of Spectatus and Firmus who both order the issue of grain, the latter to legionary soldiers. This would seem to make an identification of the Spectatus and Firmus of tablet

---

[6] Harris, *The Inscribed Economy*, pp. 12, 18 and 27.
[7] K. Hopkins, 'Rome, Taxes, Rents and Trade,' in W. Scheidel and S. von Reden (eds), *The Ancient Economy* (Edinburgh, 2002), pp. 190–230.
[8] For the convenience of the reader, the official translations of the published editions of the tablets will be appended below at the beginning of each specific case study.
[9] *Tab.Vindol.* II, p. 324; with amendment in ll. 40–41 from the Appendix of *Tab.Vindol.* III, pp. 159–60.
[10] *Tab.Vindol.* II, p. 322; for instance, two owners of the name are identified as *optio* and slave, respectively.
[11] *Tab.Vindol.* II, p. 322; and treated in *VRR* I, pp. 108–12.

343 with the pair of officers in tablet **180** likely.

The tablets have been dated collectively to Period IV, that is, the years *c*. AD 105–20, the time associated with the second occupancy of the 1st Cohort of Tungrians. Candidus must, judging from the narrative of tablet **343**, have been able to communicate easily with Spectatus and Firmus, which implies that Candidus was a resident at Vindolanda and that he was on friendly terms with at least two lower rank officers of the 1st Cohort of Tungrians. If we add to this the fact that the tablet was found inside the fort in quarters presumably occupied by a centurion, it would, indeed, seem likely that Candidus was himself a centurion or of similar status.

Returning to the contents of the letter, Octavius starts out by referring in a very general way to a transaction with a certain Marinus, who may have sold him 100 pounds of sinew. Even though no more can be inferred about this transaction, the bare mention of the commodity is interesting enough, as the sinew was presumably purchased with an eye to selling it on to the Roman army for use with artillery equipment.[12]

By far the biggest and most important transaction mentioned in the letter is, however, the purchase, on deposit of a security of 300 *denarii*, by Octavius of 5,000 *modii* of 'ears of grain' or spelt wheat, *spica*,[13] (that is 8.62 litres of grain times 5,000 = 43,100 litres of grain) which he stands to lose if he does not receive at least 500 *denarii*.[14] Just how much 5,000 *modii* of spelt is, may be conveyed by the fact that a day's energy requirement for a very active man is met by a wheat equivalent of 1/7 *modius*.[15] The amount of grain bought, therefore, represents something like 35,000 daily rations if spelt was the sole source of nourishment.

Furthermore, Octavius would not only lose his deposit, but he would also be embarrassed, *erubescam*,[16] which was put down as a concern on a par with losing his money. This is interesting, because it tells us that it was important for him to guard his reputation, but also that good credentials were no use if you had nothing to pay with. Be that as it may, what is truly significant here is, firstly, the investment in such a large quantity of grain for processing and then for selling it on to some large recipient, and, secondly, the evidence this transaction gives us of a ready and easy use of cash: this seems to have been a monetised economic system where cash was at least as important as status.

The next part of the letter concerns a specific body of hides that were stored at *Cataractonium* (Catterick).[17] Interestingly, excavations at this site have provided what appears to be firm evidence of large-scale tanning activity which fits well with the narrative of tablet **343**.[18] Now, Octavius instructed his friend to send a letter to *Cataractonium*, so that he himself could gain possession of the hides when he would see fit to go and collect them. On the basis of this bit of information, we must conclude that Octavius had neither direct ownership of the hides nor the legal status to have them 'released from custody.'

Why could this be? Either because Candidus was the legal owner of the goods, or because Candidus had a military status that gave him influence on the state-owned tanneries. However, Candidus was apparently supposed to supply a specific wagon (cf. 'the wagon about which you write' and 'write to me what is with that wagon'),[19] whereas Octavius was hesitant to expose draught animals in his own keeping to the hazards of bad weather ('I did not care to injure the animals while the roads are bad').[20] Accordingly, this seems to concern private transport, or contracting, and not official state transport—although there is, in fact, plenty of evidence in the tablets for military use of wagons, whether it be by requisition or not.[21]

Then, out of the blue, Candidus was told to confer with a third party, Tertius, about a sum of money, 8½ *denarii*, which he had received on behalf of Octavius from a fourth party, Fatalis, but not yet 'credited to his account.' The clause in question—*non illos mi accepto tulit*—is obscure, but no matter how it is to be reconstructed and interpreted, there is little reason to doubt that Tertius had

---

[12] Although no remains of siege engines have been unearthed, projectiles that might be the heads of ballista bolts have been found; see R. Birley, *The Small Finds. Fascicule I. The Weapons*, Vindolanda Research Reports, New Series, IV (Hexham 1996), pp. 8–9.

[13] Emmer wheat, *bracis*, had been the most important Celtic Iron Age crop, but was susceptible to frost and not well suited for heavy soils. Spelt wheat, *spica*, was hardier and could be sown in autumn whereby a better harvest could be obtained; the use of spelt probably increased during the Roman period. See J. Wacher, *A Portrait of Roman Britain* (London, 2000), pp. 27, 47. However, in J. Pearce, 'Food as Substance and Symbol in the Roman Army: A Case Study from Vindolanda,' in P. Freeman, J. Bennet, Z. T. Fiema and B. Hoffmann (eds), *Limes XVIII. Proceedings of the XVIIIth International Congress of Roman Frontier Studies Held in Amman, Jordan (September 2000)*, Vol. II, BAR International Series 1084 (II) (Oxford, 2002), p. 934, the identification of *bracis* with emmer is problematised, and it is suggested that *bracis* is threshed spelt, whereas *spica* is unthreshed. However, for ease of use Wacher's definitions (which are similar to those of Bowman and Thomas) are employed, bearing in mind that they may be faulty—the important thing is, however, that both words denote wheat grain.

[14] The original wording used to denote the transaction was: *tibi scripseram spicas me emisse*; *Tab.Vindol.* II.343, l. 7.

[15] *Tab.Vindol.* II, pp. 122–23.

[16] *Tab.Vindol.* II.343, ll. 13–14.

[17] See map, chapter six, p. 46. The archaeological record on the supply of leather at Vindolanda is ambiguous: based on the evidence of tentage it is difficult to argue for any shortage, but the apparent use and repair of footwear until completely worn out indicates otherwise; see C. van Driel-Murray et al., *Preliminary Reports on the Leather, Textiles, Environmental Evidence and Dendrochronology*, Vindolanda Research Reports, New Series, III (Hexham, 1993), p. 55; this work cited hereafter as *VRR* III.

[18] *Tab.Vindol.* II, p. 322; and Frere, *Britannia*, p. 216.

[19] *Tab.Vindol.* II.343, l. 17f: *karrum de quo scribis*; l. 18f: *quit sit cum eo karro mi scribe*; respectively.

[20] *Tab.Vindol.* II.343, l. 20f: *iumenta non curaui uexsare dum uiae male sunt*.

[21] See esp. *Tab.Vindol.* II.314–16. At Bu Njem, the transportation of grain supplies was carried out by civilian contractors: *O.Bu.Njem* 76–80.

the money and that he had not made any arrangements for returning it to its rightful owner, Octavius.[22] Once again, we witness how ubiquitous the use of cash was: the value of the purchase of grain concerned at least 800 *denarii*, and here we see the same man going to some lengths to retrieve one hundredth of that amount.

The narrative so far has been concerned with the topics which were of most importance to Octavius and his, we might say, 'business associate:' things to be done immediately and things to be taken care of along the way. But now, on the third piece of tablet, he goes on to account for the state of their apparently shared business. Octavius had finished tanning 170 hides and threshing 119 *modii* of emmer wheat, *bracis*, and now his activities had ground to a halt due to lack of grain to process. He repeats his appeals to Candidus to send money, so that the purchase of the new, large amount of grain could go through, and so that he could continue his threshing activity.

This attitude towards buying, processing and (what he does not mention) selling, seems to imply a decidedly 'entrepreneurial' frame of mind: Octavius was in charge of a 'business' which was a specialised means of production, and which he did not want to see, or could not afford to see, out of work. He was not a miller who leant back and waited for his customers to come to him, but an active agent who bought up grain and processed it as *one part only* of his business activities. For, of course, we know that he was also engaged in the sale of sinew and the processing of leather goods, which are entirely different kinds of commodities and trades.

This tanning business is also what the last part of the letter is concerned with: the sale of hides. On the face of it, a potential buyer, who was a friend of a friend (*contubernalis Fronti amici*),[23] had shown up and had wanted to buy a consignment of hides,[24] and an agreement was made: Octavius promised a deadline for delivery of the goods, 1st March, and the buyer in turn promised to come back on 13th January. These dates make no sense if they concerned a simple 'buying-and-selling' process: why would the client return one and a half months before his goods were ready for sale? However, a few lines further down on tablet-piece number four, we learn that this potential buyer never actually paid any money. It would therefore seem likely that the two first met and entered into a verbal business agreement, and that the buyer was then to return in the middle of January to pay, or at least to lay down a deposit, for his goods, which he would then receive on 1st March.

As it was, Frontius' messmate did not return, and the sale did not go through, but Octavius added two comments:

firstly, that the buyer did not show up again because he already had hides, and secondly that he, Octavius, would have done business if only he had received the money. The first comment implies both that Octavius had good 'intelligence' of his customers and that he considered it relevant to know why one of his customers would back out of a deal (he had apparently been supplied by a competitor), and the second comment seems to bear on the 'social politics' of business—it was not Octavius' fault that the sale did not go through, and he was therefore not to blame for turning down one of his friend Frontius' messmates.

Most importantly though, it is worth remarking on the similarities between the way that Octavius and this *contubernalis* acted as economic agents: they both readily entered into agreements that they did not necessarily intend to go through with or were capable of honouring. Their activities resemble 'business' where dealings are determined by cash and the quest for a quick profit, rather than socially embedded trade where a deal is sealed and kept on the basis of a man's word of honour. For these two people, at least, money would seem to have weighed heavier than status and reputation.

In the above, I mentioned that Octavius had seemed to be aware of and concerned with competition. This point is further underlined by the closing sentence of the narrative, where Octavius informed Candidus that a certain Frontinius Julius was selling on 'at a high price for leather-working' some goods that he had obtained from him at a lower price.[25] In other words, he was reporting directly to his associate about the dealings of a client and would-be competitor, and one that appeared to be making a profit out of his dealings with them. Once again, we witness how inherent the idea of making money was for the protagonists in this letter: there is no trace of incentives other than a profit-motive.

In the closing greeting of the letter, where Octavius asked his friend to convey his greetings to named persons, we also find the somewhat extraneous final remark that he had 'received letters from Gleuco.'[26] We do not know who Gleuco was, or what the letters might have been about, but it is interesting in so far as it serves as additional evidence of Octavius' wide-flung network of friends, business partners and clients—no less than ten different people are mentioned in a letter of no great length.

It is crucial here to emphasise the aggregate evidence for Octavius' civilian status, or for the circumstance that he was conducting business in a private capacity: the letter mentions that Octavius—without there being any hint suggesting that he was working as a 'quartermaster' or dispatched on 'commissariat duties'—purchased grain

---

[22] *Tab.Vindol.* II.343, l. 23; 'he has not credited them to my account,' as Bowman and Thomas have chosen to translate it, may imply more complex credit operations than were actually the case.
[23] *Tab.Vindol.* II.343, l. 29f.
[24] At least, that is the most plausible meaning of the ambiguous Latin phrase: *desiderabat coria ei adsignarem et ita denarios daturus erat*; *Tab.Vindol.* II.343, l. 31.
[25] Tab.*Vindol.* II.343, l.38: *Frontinium Julium audio magno licere pro coriatione*. The meaning of the phrase *pro coriatione* is open to interpretation—the above is the translation provided in the Appendix of *Tab.Vindol.* III, p. 159.
[26] *Tab.Vindol.* II.343, l. 44.

and was about to lose money and be embarrassed; that Octavius could not himself get hides from *Cataractonium*, and that he and Candidus were to supply the wagon and draught animals themselves; that somebody owed Octavius, personally, an amount of money; that he, not anybody under his command, had finished tanning and threshing; that he would freely have given hides for money; and finally, it was of interest to both Octavius and Candidus that a third party was profiting from his dealings with them. This may seem to be a tedious listing of points already treated, but in my opinion it leaves little room for interpretations suggesting that Octavius might have been an officer or similar acting in an official capacity.[27] Civilians (who could, however, be discharged veterans) must have had any number of personal- or business reasons to fraternise with soldiers or officers, so we should not force readings favouring direct army involvement where it does not, in fact, appear to be evident.[28]

In conclusion, tablet **343** provides very significant evidence of the nature of Roman trade in a frontier zone, if not of Roman trade in general: this kind of economic activity was characterised by entrepreneurial, profit-motivated individuals who did business, cooperated and competed according to the specific circumstances of each transaction. Someone who was apparently a civilian trader could be business partner with a military officer, and they could pool their assets and capabilities in order to make a profit out of whatever opportunities presented themselves—be that supplying the army and deriving advantages from its manufacturing facilities, business with other entrepreneurs, or possibly even trade with local natives. In this way, state redistribution, through the spending of tax money, became the economic driving force behind private enterprise in the frontier zone, which in this case caused the production and circulation of sinew, grain (spelt as well as emmer) and leather goods.[29]

Tab.Vindol. II.**344**, in translation:

> ... he beat (?) me all the more ... goods ... or pour them down the drain (?). As befits an honest man (?) I implore your majesty not to allow me, an innocent man, to have been beaten with rods and, my lord, inasmuch as (?) I was unable to complain to the prefect because he was detained by ill-health I have complained in vain (?) to the *beneficiarius* and the rest (?) of the centurions of his (?) unit. Accordingly (?) I implore your mercifulness not to allow me, a man from overseas and an innocent one, about whose good faith you may inquire, to have been bloodied by rods as if I had committed some crime.[30]

The above narrative was found on the backside of tablet **180**, written in the same hand as tablets **180** and **181** and discovered together with these and tablet **343** (all mentioned above).[31] Therefore, this unfortunate 'man from overseas' (*homo tra<n>smarinus*),[32] must be the same person who distributed grain to Candidus, Spectatus and Firmus (among others), and who made an account of sales and debts where Candidus might be figuring for a second time. Accordingly, tablet **344** was also found in relation to what is considered to have been a centurion's quarters. Significantly, the *Dura-Europus* archive of military documents contains two official rulings on commercial issues by a local tribune, so although the context is quite different here—seeing as the tablets in question are a letter, two accounts and a petition—Roman officers may have had more reason to concern themselves with the humdrum proceedings of daily trade than is otherwise often assumed.[33]

Even though any specific identification of the author of the tablet is impossible, the few personal details he reveals here give us invaluable information about the context of the other accounts he wrote. For here we have a letter which can be interpreted as something akin to solid evidence of a civilian trader involved in economic activity at Vindolanda:[34] first of all, the narrative itself implies that it was written by a civilian—it mentions 'innocence' (*innocens*), 'crime' (*scelus*) and having been 'bloodied by rods' (*virgis cruentatum esse*) in a way that an auxiliary soldier would not have done,[35] and the 'quality of the Latinity' is remarkable;[36] second, the petitioner is complaining about a beating, which, again, an ordinary, auxiliary soldier would not, but which a Roman citizen with legal rights certainly would, and the letter seems to mention the loss of a commodity or merchandise, *merx*,[37] which further implies that he might well have been a trader; third, instead of acting according to any established, official rules of complaining or petitioning, like a soldier or officer would do,[38] the writer

---

[27] *Contra* A. R. Birley, *Garrison Life*, p. 114.
[28] Cf. also *Tab.Vindon.* 46 which attests to close ties between the fort and surrounding villas, or the motley assortment of private letters by soldiers, miners and civilians, concerning procurement of various desirable goods, constituted by *O.Claud.* I.137–47, 150–78.
[29] Cf. C. R. Whittaker, *Frontiers of the Roman Empire: A Social and Economic Study* (Baltimore, MD; and London, 1994), p. 113.
[30] *Tab.Vindol.* II, p. 331.
[31] Bowman and Thomas are quite sure about the shared origin of these three tablets; *Tab.Vindol.* II, p. 329.
[32] *Tab.Vindol.* II.344, l. 15.
[33] The documents in question are *P.Dura-Europus* 125 (freeing a third party from his obligation to guarantee the validity of contract—maybe to ensure against any hidden defects in a traded slave) and 126 (concerning the division of a potter's shop).
[34] *Contra* R. Birley, *Vindolanda: Extraordinary Records of Daily Life on the Northern Frontier* (Greenhead, 2005), p. 95.
[35] Quotes from *Tab.Vindol.* II.344, ll. 16, 18 and 17, respectively.
[36] So remark Bowman and Thomas, *Tab.Vindol.* II, p. 330.
[37] *Tab.Vindol.* II.344, l. 2.
[38] Compare the unofficial and personal nature of this letter with the official petitions of ordinary soldiers applying to the prefect for leave, *Tab.Vindol.* II.166–76.

instead tries to get through to the prefect himself and then goes on to complain to various centurions and the *beneficiarius*—a type of officer which recent research suggests acted as a link between the financial authorities of the province and the administrative staffs of military units by controlling commercial traffic and inspecting commodities transported, some of which were military supplies;[39] and finally, the letter is written in a tone which implies that the petitioner was not part of the military community, for instead of emphasising any military rank, status or connections, he chooses to identify himself as *transmarinus* (which would be an odd thing for a Tungrian soldier to do), maybe indicating that he is a provincial from Gaul or even from one of the core provinces.

Interestingly, we have comparable evidence for civilians petitioning in this way: a stone-mason from *Mons Claudianus* wrote to the local *beneficiarius* through his centurion, requesting the former to hand over a petition to the faraway prefect in charge.[40] In contrast, an unknown Vindolandan soldier under severe accusation of some crime handled things rather differently—unlike the 'man from overseas,' he chose to act within the social structure of the military community:

> —my mistake(?), whose help I am also (?) asking for(?) to no purpose. So please believe me that I retire thus so that my reputation is intact, which is the chief point.[41]

> And yet I want it to be clear to you that I am withdrawing neither from the mess nor from the club unless ... to the chief. But he saw me, perhaps(?), at the goldsmiths' or the silversmiths' and this is...[42]

> —if anyone has said that I ... the mess ... Greet from me Rhenus, Felicio, (?), Tetricus ...[43]

Thus, these three fragments highlight how a soldier or lower officer, who held a position in the cohort's internal hierarchy, would go about defending himself and attempting to clear his name by drawing on the support of friends and messmates.[44]

However, returning once again to the contents of tablet **344,** the nature of the goods in question must remain an open question, for the use of the verb *effundere* (to pour out) does not necessarily imply that we are talking about liquid commodities such as fish-sauce or wine, since the same term can be applied to the motion of grain being poured away.[45] As regards the identity of the man whose help and protection he was seeking, some would have it that the use of the title *tua maiestas*[46] within Period IV (*c.* AD 105–120) implies that he was invoking the mercy of the Emperor Hadrian himself—but it could be anybody of high standing.[47] Likewise, a petition dating from Period III (*c.* AD 97/100–105) reveals how an unknown writer (who may have been the previous commander at Vindolanda) implored the then prefect, Flavius Cerialis, to continue keeping somebody in custody whom the writer had treated badly earlier and whose wrath he now feared.[48]

To sum up, the value of tablet **344** lies in the positive identification of a civilian entrepreneur at Vindolanda, and, furthermore, one who can be traced through other tablets to have been active both in the official administration and distribution of military food supplies (we will return to tablet **180** below, p. 27), and in selling various goods for cash and on credit to individual members of the military community, ranging from the rank and file to a centurion.

Tab.Vindol. III.**645**, in translation:

> Maior to his Maritimus, greetings. I wanted you to know that a letter has been sent to me by my father in which he writes to me that I should make known to him what I shall have done about ... But if you have conducted business in that regard(?) with the *Caesariani*, see that you write back to me with clear information so that I can write back to this effect to my father. If you have made any payment from time to time, I shall remove grain[49] from store(?) for you without delay in proportion to the sum which may be raised. When I was writing this to you, I was making the bed warm. I wish you may enjoy the best of fortune. ... sends you greetings. Farewell. (Margin) If you intend to send a boy to

---

[39] See C. C. Monfort, 'The Roman Military Supply During the Principate. Transportation and Staples,' in P. Erdkamp (ed.), *The Roman Army and the Economy* (Amsterdam, 2002), pp. 77–79.
[40] *O.Claud.* IV.868.
[41] *Tab.Vindol.* III.655B.
[42] *Tab.Vindol.* III.656.
[43] *Tab.Vindol.* III.657A–B.
[44] The unknown writer is also the author of *Tab.Vindol.* III.346: a letter accompanying a package of garments for a friend and containing greetings for one or more of the messmates mentioned in *Tab.Vindol.* III.657B.
[45] *Tab.Vindol.* II.344, l. 3.
[46] *Tab.Vindol.* II.344, l. 4.
[47] *Contra* A. R. Birley, *Garrison Life*, p. 117.
[48] *Tab.Vindol.* II.256.
[49] Note that the Latin reads *bracis* (*Tab.Vindol.* III.645, l. 14), which means that a more correct translation would be either 'emmer,' 'threshed spelt' or 'wheat,' and not 'grain' more generally, as Bowman and Thomas have chosen to render it; see above p. 16, n. 13.

me(?), send a note of hand with him so that I may be the more reassured.

(Back) [Deliver] at Vindolanda. To Cocceiius Maritimus from Maior.[50]

This tablet has been dated to Period III, *c.* AD 97/100–105, and together with Octavius' letter to Candidus, tablet **343**, it is the only surviving longer narrative relating directly to mercantile activity. Tablet **645** is a letter written by a man named Maior to his associate Maritimus, but it is impossible to say very much about either person's work status: they could both have been civilians or soldiers, or soldiers acting as private individuals. However, they both bore Roman names and so we might assume that they were Roman citizens.

Maior's reason for writing was that he himself had received a letter from his father, in which the father enquired about his son's activities in relation to what is either to be interpreted as 'the spindle <of a mill>' or 'the spilled <grain>.'[51] Apparently, this induced Maior to write and ask of Maritimus whether he had done any business, *negotium*,[52] concerning this matter with the *Caesariani*, that is, the emperor's slaves and freedmen who were employed empire-wide in administrative and tax-collection duties.[53] This anticipated business with the *Caesariani* seems to have been a costly matter, for Maior promised to repay immediately, with grain from his own store, any outlays made by Maritimus.

Accordingly, this 'business' which Maritimus was to conduct on Maior's behalf would appear to have involved 'processed grain' of some sort (either the process of milling grain or threshed grain as a commodity) and some kind of sought after agreement with state officials. Furthermore, it is evident that Maior already had emmer, *bracis*, so either he wanted to sell threshed or milled *bracis* to the *Caesariani* or he wanted to pay Maritimus in *bracis* for obtaining an agreement with the *Caesariani* about the purchase of *spica*, that is spelt. The exact nature of the transaction remains unknown to us, though.

However, the important thing for present purposes is that the letter obviously concerns commerce, more specifically something to do with grain, and that this was a transaction between no less than four parties: father, son, agent and officials. The way Maior's father was concerned about his son's doings implies that this was a family business where Maior was but the second, albeit active, link in the enterprise. As a family business concerned with grain trade, this must be more evidence of private commercial activity, the unknown status of Maior aside.

Cocceiius Maritimus, however, was apparently resident at Vindolanda, and there is a greater likelihood that he was a soldier or government employee, especially in light of the fact that he was in contact with the *Caesariani*.[54] He was apparently acting as an agent for Maior using connections particular to his own person or circumstances, and could pay for expenses that he was expected to incur in the process, which implies that he had private means.[55] Furthermore, Maritimus was not to be repaid in cash, but in *bracis*, which makes sense only if he conducted commercial activities of his own whereby he could dispose of the grain for cash himself. Lastly, we can infer from the fact that he was to 'send a boy,' that is, a slave,[56] with his answer that this was not military business, in which case an official messenger (a soldier) could have been used,[57] or that Maritimus was indeed civilian.

In conclusion, the value of tablet **645** lies in the evidence it gives of private, in this case family, business, the use of agents and the link between private commerce and the redistributive system of the Roman state and military supply.

Evidence drawn from miscellaneous tablets
In the above, three examples of well preserved writing-tablets pertaining to trade or market activity have been dealt with in detail through a case-by-case analysis. However, most of the Vindolanda material concerning economic activity is much more fragmented, ambiguous and scattered, but when combined it still constitutes a sizeable *corpus* of useful evidence. What follows, therefore, is a summary account based on what these tablets have to say about market activity in Roman Britain.[58]

First of all, it is worth remarking on the different types of market transactions recorded in the tablets: sales and purchases, debts and repayments, purchases on credit and the use of deposits. Some of these transactional relationships, it might be argued, are not *necessarily* subject to the conditions of market-mediated exchange, but the point is that the transactions of which we have evidence in the Vindolanda Tablets *do*, in fact, appear to have been concluded within the overall framework of the market. Specifically, the most relevant evidence is constituted by what appears to be traders' lists of sales, debts, and repayments (as signified by the 'crossing out' or 'checking off' of the entry with the name of the debtor and his debt), and tablets referring to the actual process of

---

[50] *Tab.Vindol.* III, p. 100.
[51] *Tab.Vindol.* III.645, ll. 6-7: *de fussa*; but see also *Tab.Vindol.* III, p. 101, note on ll. 6–8.
[52] *Tab.Vindol.* III.645, l. 8.
[53] A. R. Birley, *Garrison Life*, p. 118.
[54] Bowman and Thomas would have it that his *gentilicium*, Cocceiius, could suggest that he was a freedman of Nerva, either an administrator or a soldier; *Tab.Vindol.* III, p. 100.
[55] *Internumeraveris* is taken by the editors to mean 'payment from time to time,' see Appendix of *Tab.Vindol.* III, p. 101, note on ll. 12–13.
[56] The Latin is *puer*, which in Classical Latin is often—and certainly in a context like this—supposed to denominate a household slave; *Tab.Vindol.* III.645, 'Margin.'
[57] As in *Tab.Vindol.* II.252: *per equitem ad te misi* (l. ii.1–2).
[58] A glance at the Appendix provides the reader an easy way of getting a simplified overview.

buying and selling.⁵⁹

The alternative is to argue that all prices agreed between traders or entrepreneurs and the military occupants of the fort were determined by social relations and a sort of 'moral economy.'⁶⁰ Moreover, the same applies to the two large business deals attested in tablets **343** and **645**: there is no reason why these entrepreneurs should not have been using, and also themselves have been subject to, the price-making mechanism of the market. At least, no hint of evidence exists in these two tablets as to extra-economic considerations or obligations that were paramount to what can be termed 'normal business.' This is not to say that social and political factors did not play a role in each transaction, just to say that this did not in itself move the transactions out of the realm of market-mediated exchange and into a parallel economic dimension of redistribution or reciprocity.

So, leaving aside the exact type of exchange for a moment, how were these transactions facilitated? By barter, payment in kind or payment in cash? The overall impression is that the predominant method, by a considerable margin, was payment in cash—all the tablets mentioned up until now have dealt with and listed transactions in cash. There were, however, a few transactions conducted in other ways: in tablet **182** there are two instances of transactions involving barter, and these along with tablet **645**, already mentioned, which speaks of payment in kind for services provided as a sort of business agent, are the only cases of payment in kind that can be identified in all of the tablets with any certainty.⁶¹ Otherwise, every single transaction was measured in terms of cash and paid for with money. It would seem, therefore, that an extensive, working cash economy was firmly in place at Vindolanda; or at least, to be more precise, *within* the walls of Vindolanda, for we have very little evidence which does not solely concern the military inhabitants of the fort.⁶²

However, one highly significant characteristic of this Vindolandan cash economy is worth remarking on: the types of coin in use. If one analyses the *corpus* of tablets, it is possible to make a list in excess of 500 more or less well-identified transactions, and out of these there are eighty-nine with a surviving price in *denarii* but only twenty-nine which do not include fractions of *denarii* or *asses*.⁶³ Moreover, the 'median,'⁶⁴ that is to say, the most commonly traded amount, of the payments made in *denarii* is 2.5 and for *asses* the median is 2. In light of the fact that 'the more or less substantial presence of coins of very low value is an indicator of the level of monetisation,'⁶⁵ what are we to conclude when two thirds of all transactions implicitly involved *sestertii* (¼ of a *denarius*) or the low denomination copper *as* (1/16 of a *denarius*); that most recorded transactions were rather low-value anyway; and that payment in cash was absolutely paramount compared to any other kind of exchange?

Probably that the economy of Vindolanda was subject to some very specific circumstances, namely that more than five hundred soldiers within the fort received a nominal payment of 250 *denarii* per person per year, and that they did not have a lot of opportunities to spend that money elsewhere.⁶⁶ This is a statement with two important qualifications, though: firstly, as much as two thirds of that pay was docked for mandatory disbursements of food, equipment, etc.,⁶⁷ and secondly, several tablets attest to soldiers applying for leave, *commeatus*, in nearby towns—hence, they would have spent part of their salaries in other places.⁶⁸ This being said, however, the soldiers do seem to have had a fair amount of cash at their disposal: tablets **650** and **655** attest to individuals transferring cash between one another, and from further afield similar evidence crop up at the western end of the Stanegate, in *Luguvalium* (present-day Carlisle), while a formal 'contract' from *Vindonissa* attests to soldiers lending money at interest between themselves.⁶⁹ Finally, a well-preserved tablet recording the payment of a cavalryman, also from *Vindonissa*, reveals that he had 50 *denarii* paid out to him, with written guarantee of a further 75 *denarii* to be paid out as his next salary.⁷⁰

Since cash was abundant and a lot of goods were beyond the manufacturing capabilities of the fort's skilled labourers themselves and army supply in general, one would imagine that the few relatively luxurious or normally unobtainable items that were marketed by traders or entrepreneurs extraneous to the military community could have been sold at advantageous prices —in other words, that a large demand and inflexible lack of supply would have led to a kind of 'boom town' economy. Yet, this was not a rapacious seller's market,

---

⁵⁹ For lists of sales etc., see *Tab.Vindol.* II.181, 182, 184, IV.i.861; and for letters referring to the buying and selling of goods, see *Tab.Vindol.* II.213, 343, 348, III.646.
⁶⁰ Cf. E. P. Thompson, 'The Moral Economy of the English Crowd in the Eighteenth Century,' in *Past & Present*, 50 (1971), 78–79, 108, 112.
⁶¹ There are other examples of transactions in kind, but I would argue that these are cases of reciprocity, not market exchange; see chapter five.
⁶² However, *Tab.Vindol.*II.178 is an account of the 'daily revenues of the fort' listing a daily income in cash, and thus, it might imply that the local civilians paid in coin and not in kind.
⁶³ And some of these prices might actually have had a fractional value attached which is lost to us, as many of the tablets are missing their right margins.
⁶⁴ From statistics: the figure in the middle of a row of numbers with as many lower figures as higher ones.
⁶⁵ Andreau, *Banking and Business*, p. 147.
⁶⁶ That is, a legionary received 1200 *sestertii* during the reign of Domitian (AD 71–96), see R. Duncan-Jones, *The Economy of the Roman Empire: Quantitative Studies* (Cambridge, 1974), p. 10; however, auxiliaries were only paid 5/6 of legionaries, that is 250 *denarii*, see Erdkamp, 'Introduction,' p. 7.
⁶⁷ Cf. J. R. Rodriguez, 'Baetica and Germania. Notes on the Concept of "Provincial Interdependence" in the Roman Empire,' in P. Erdkamp (ed.), *The Roman Army and the Economy* (Amsterdam, 2002), p. 296.
⁶⁸ Cf. *Tab.Vindol.* II.166–77.
⁶⁹ Respectively: *Tab.Vindol.* III.650 (which may not be very representative, however), 655; *Tab.Luguval.* 29; *Tab.Vindon.* 3.
⁷⁰ *Tab.Vindon.* 4, ll. 3–4.

which implies that the fort must have been quite well integrated within a wider economic framework of exchange. This is an important finding, and it is supplemented by the original numismatic survey of J. P. Casey who concluded that 'very considerable sums of money were normally handled on the site' and that the value of coins found in areas of different social significance (barracks, *praetoria* and other places) did not differ.[71]

It is evident, then, that a substantial amount of cash-facilitated market trading was going on at Vindolanda. The next question that arises is to what extent the military community was economically integrated into a wider market involving its own hinterland? First of all, it is important to point out that the evidence from various traders' lists of sales and debts seems to speak of a class of mobile, civilian, Roman traders and entrepreneurs selling everything from towels to horses—and we know that at least one of these traders was from overseas. Although this is positive evidence of an intermittent integration into a regional or even provincial trading network, it is also negative evidence of significant integration into a local, Romano-British market economy supplying all kinds of goods and wares—if either the native hinterland or fort *territorium* could have supplied these commodities, they would have done so. In addition, this view is supported by another piece of negative evidence for significant integration in a wider market for commercial goods: the chronic lack of footwear attested at Vindolanda (particularly in the first four periods), in light of the fact that finds on the Rhine frontier indicate that shoes were in plentiful supply there.[72]

However, there is nonetheless evidence of at least one kind of commercial relationship with the surrounding area: that of the purchase and sale of different kinds of grain and food in general—of what one might call 'perishables.' The existence of a local market for farm produce is probably best attested by quoting some relevant tablets:

> Curtius Super to his Cassius, greetings. ... so that you may explain and so that they may get from you barley as commercial goods ... (Back) To Cassius Saecularis.[73]
>
> ... to have done ... about the *braces*, which you are assigning (?) for sale ...[74]
> Montanus to Optatus, his brother(?), greetings ... if you will have had the opportunity of selling ...

I pray that you are in good health (Back) [Deliver at] Vindolanda. To Optatus the maltster from Montanus, his brother.[75]

> ... bruised beans, two *modii*, chickens, twenty, a hundred apples, if you can find nice ones, a hundred or two hundred eggs, if they are for sale there at a fair price. ... 8 *sextarii* of fish-sauce ... a *modius* of olives ... (Back) To ... slave (?) of Verecundus.[76]

Now, if we consider these four examples along with the evidence for entrepreneurial purchase and processing of grain found in tablets **343** and **645**, then it would seem that there is, indeed, a strong case to argue for the existence of a market for agricultural products. Even if all six tablets involve military personnel in some fashion or other, be it in a private or official capacity, it remains impossible to class these transactions as simple redistribution—although they may concern trade with surplus goods obtained through the command economy. In particular, a certain officer, Cassius Saecularis, is attested as having acted as agent and possibly interpreter (*ut interpreteris*),[77] implying business with natives, in the sale of a consignment of barley in tablet **213**, quoted above, and he was involved in some sort of deal involving military supplies of wood and timber, as well.[78]

The fourth of the above examples, tablet **302**, which seems to be a grocery list of the prefect of the 1st Cohort of Tungrians (occupancy *c.* AD 85–92), is highly interesting because it lists everything from common farm products of a rather perishable nature (apples as well as eggs) to somewhat exotic and certainly imported goods such as fish-sauce and olives. And yet, this is not a list of supplies received, for it is evident from the text itself that the alleged slave was on an errand as a potential buyer—maybe to a larger commercial centre in connection with one of the bigger military establishments such as *Coria* (Corbridge).[79]

Accordingly, there seems to have been two different kinds of market exchange working across the fort-hinterland divide: that of mobile, civilian traders supplying all kinds of different goods, as long as the price was high enough to make the transportation worthwhile, but whom we cannot ascribe to any specific region or social network (the evidence is simply too scarce); and that of a local market for agricultural produce catering for the basic as well as more sophisticated needs of the fort and possibly buying up some of the garrison's surplus

---

[71] Cf. *VRR* I, p. 144.
[72] Cf. *VRR* III, pp. 34–35.
[73] *Tab.Vindol.* II.213, l. ii.2–3: *ut hordeum commercium habeant a te*.
[74] *Tab.Vindol.* II.348, l. 2f: *adscribis vendendam*.
[75] *Tab.Vindol.* III.646, ll. 6–7: *si habueris occas[sionem] vendendi*.
[76] *Tab.Vindol.* II.302, l. 5: *si ibi aequo emantur*.
[77] *Tab.Vindol.* II.213, l. ii.1.
[78] *Tab.Vindol.* II.215.
[79] See map, chapter six, p. 46.

grain-supplies, as well.[80] Interestingly, we find that there was also a thriving exchange of homegrown garden produce at the combined military- and mining outpost of *Mons Claudianus* in Egypt—even despite its arid location in the middle of the eastern desert.[81]

As should already be apparent, the scope of the market—that is, the variety of goods and types of transactions conducted within this economic framework—was impressive and multi-faceted. Just a short and selective list of goods paid or owed for by residents at Vindolanda encompasses examples ranging from apples and eggs to bedspreads and tunics, iron, timber, spears, fish-sauce, salt and, to round off, even pepper and olives![82] The value of this plentiful, literary evidence for the actual objects of trade is underlined by comparison with Strabo's short 'list of exports' (cf. above, p. 9) which only mentions that 'It [the isle of Britain] produces corn, cattle, gold, silver and iron. These things are exported along with hides, slaves and dogs, suitable for hunting.'[83] Tacitus is even less informative in telling us that Britain was 'tolerant of crops and prolific of cattle,' that it produced 'gold, and silver and other metals' and that 'their sea also produces pearls.'[84] In short, the tablets augment our knowledge in a major way, revealing to us how people were buying simple as well as more luxurious food, textiles, livestock, tools and equipment.

The point to be made is that things were being purchased or sold through market exchange which we would not normally, at a Roman fort, expect to find under this category—most notably grain and weapons. This is significant because of the simple fact that we would imagine the relevant military needs for these goods to be supplied through redistributive channels. Contrast, for instance, the sale of spears as well as more mundane items (towels, cloaks, etc.) to individual soldiers in tablet **861** with the official supply of weapons to a cavalry unit attested at *Luguvalium* (Carlisle) (treated below, p. 29): in the former, goods are purchased by the soldiers themselves (paid or owed for), while an officer is requisitioning the weapons for his men seemingly free of charge in the latter. Thus, when we do find these commodities being made the objects of trade, we need to reconsider seriously both the roles hitherto attributed to individual agents and the overall system of economic activities in general.

This is further borne out by the range of 'market relationships' we find in the tablets, which include: soldiers buying from traders; private individuals acting as agents for one another; (overseas) traders involved in administering state supplies; entrepreneurs making business contacts with state officials; and entrepreneurs buying up basic commodities, processing, manufacturing and selling again. Taking this complex web of economic relationships and activities into consideration (both of which we can only rarely map out in their entirety on the basis of the tablets alone), it does indeed seem correct that 'in a highly hierarchized society such as Rome, several levels of financial activity existed, linked to the multiple strata of statuses and circles.'[85] It is significant, however, that whereas the author of this quotation was speaking in a tentative manner of the banking and business systems of Rome itself, the evidence accounted for in this chapter seems to imply a similar level of economic dynamism in the furthest province of the Empire, albeit on a somewhat lesser scale.[86]

Concluding remarks on market activity

Civilian entrepreneurs and traders were operating on a large scale and were routinely buying, processing, transporting and selling a wide variety of goods. Exchange was conducted through buying and selling, often on credit, at recorded prices, and in nearly all instances the exchange was facilitated by the use of standard Roman currency. Prices varied between fractions of a day's pay to huge outlays, and most transactions concerned only some three days' worth of payment, but every exchange was still meticulously recorded with its cash price.

The system of market relationships was surprisingly complex, and we learn of traders dealing freely with the rank and file of the military community as well as with its more skilled functionaries and a number of officers of different ranks. In addition, the scope of the market was extensive and included a range of commodities that one would not have expected to be objects of trade. In fact, it seems as if we might even be able to distinguish between two different markets with which the economy of Vindolanda was connected: an inter-regional, or even inter-provincial, market for all sorts of commodities which were in demand at Vindolanda and which were supplied by traders and entrepreneurs settled in, near, or with connection to the fort; and a local market for farm produce where foods of many different kinds and prices were traded, but where basic necessities may have been supplied by native farmers while the more luxurious perishables must have been supplied by unknown, professional agents. However, civilian agents or native groupings on either side of the frontier might also have participated as buyers and consumers to whom surplus grain and goods could be sold.

As discussed in the first part of this chapter, it makes no sense to try and deny the role of the market even if

---

[80] Compare this with a model of market activity in contemporary, military-occupied Wales in J. L. Davies, 'Soldiers, Peasants, Industry and Towns. The Roman Army in Britain. A Welsh Perspective,' in P. Erdkamp (ed.), *The Roman Army and the Economy* (Amsterdam, 2002), p. 196.
[81] Cf. *O.Claud.* II.224–42, 370.
[82] A comprehensive list can be found in the Appendix; spears are traded in *Tab.Vindol.* IV.i.861.
[83] Strabo, *Geographica* 4.5.2 (199).
[84] Tacitus, *Agricola*, 12.5–6.
[85] Andreau, *Banking and Business*, p. 57. Moreover, Andreau twice poses the question of 'how far those networks extended and what existed beyond them?' (*ibid.*, p. 62; see, likewise, *ibid.*, p. 132); the present study can be seen as attempting to offer a partial answer to that question.
[86] As was touched upon in the case study of *Tab.Vindol.* II.343, Octavius' letter, social networks connecting individuals involved in the exchange of goods are highly prominent in the Vindolanda Tablets, and yet more social ties are to be exposed in the following chapters. Consider also the communal spirit inherent in dedicating an altar stone as the *vicani Vindolandesses* (*RIB* I, 1700).

factors other than supply and demand alone were at work, and with that reservation in mind, it is quite impossible to relegate the evidence of widespread market activity attested by the Vindolanda Tablets to any other category: this is neither redistribution nor reciprocity—although the tablets attest that kind of economic behaviour as well, as we shall see in the following chapters. However, the implications of this particular kind of economic activity can be dealt with in full only when we have covered the roles of the two other kinds of exchange, and any more far-reaching conclusions will therefore be withheld until the general synthesis of evidence, interpretations and models in chapter six.

In conclusion, it would seem that Vindolanda was part of an economic system which featured some quite modernist traits, like entrepreneurial activity and an extensive market economy based on the ubiquitous use of cash, but which can still also be made to fit within the hazy framework of Finley's primitivist model (seeing as military establishments represented exceptions to the rule), granted that there are some strict limitations to the degree of primitive economic behaviour postulated. On the other hand, the tablets do provide strong testimony in support of the case of formalism, the existence of the market and its validity as an ancient means of exchange. Of course, the kind of evidence treated in this chapter lends itself to a formalist perspective, but there is no denying that it still constitutes plenty of good, positive evidence for market activity in general and for an accompanying (market-) economic rationality.

Chapter 4
Redistribution: No Beer, No Bravery

The concept of redistribution and political- or command economies

'Redistribution' is not a term often employed to describe economic processes, so let us start out by defining the meaning of the term and explaining its use in this study.

Polanyi defined redistribution as an economic system where 'action is instead centripetal movement of many upon one central figure followed by an initiative of that central figure upon the many.'[1] Central authority is the vital force behind this 'pull' of material means towards a centre, but it is important to emphasise that this centre itself is not an abstraction: the centre comprises a centralising figure whose authority may be grounded in religion, military prowess, wealth or common consent, but it is a fixed figure in relation to which everybody else is subordinated and bound.

The degree to which redistribution can be said to constitute the basic economic system of any given society depends on 'the extent to which the allocation of goods is collected in one hand and takes place by virtue of custom, law or *ad hoc* central decision.'[2] The basic principle is a process of collection undertaken by the administrative apparatus of the centralising figure followed by a distribution according to the say-so of this same person—whether or not the values collected ever actually reach the physical centre of power is inconsequential.

Once again, as mentioned in the previous chapter, it would be foolish to believe in the universal rule of one mode of exchange only, so instead of viewing the world of the Romans as purely redistributive, with the consuls of the Republican Era and the emperors from the Augustan Age onwards as the centralising figures, we should instead conceive of the overall economic system as a plurality of exchange processes incorporating both market exchange, reciprocity and redistribution. For the question is not whether one mode of exchange or another was in existence at any given time in antiquity, but rather how important each was relative to the others and how they interacted.[3]

Polanyi's own view of the nature of exchange within ancient society should not be forgotten either, for he explicitly claimed that:

> Redistribution, the ruling method in tribal and archaic society beside which [market] exchange plays only a minor part, grew to great importance in the later Roman Empire and is actually gaining ground today in some modern industrial states. The Soviet Union is an extreme instance.[4]

While this comparison helps us to understand better Polanyi's conception of the nature of this particular kind of exchange, it also causes one to wonder what he would have thought of the 'bail-out' strategies of the recent financial crisis and the way that modes of economic organisation have waxed and waned over the past fifty years.

With the complexities of present-day economies in mind, we should therefore take great caution not to simplify or reduce the patterns of exchange to which our scanty evidence for Roman economic activity attests. Modern 'market economies' certainly contain elements of both redistribution (government taxation and expenditure) and reciprocity (private expenditure determined by social, or more explicitly family, relations and initiatives like 'fair-trade' products). So if we seem to witness a chaotic blending of redistributive- and market exchange practices then that is no more than our own experience of economy and society should lead us to expect.

As regards the Roman Empire, there are some striking redistributive traits that have been described again and again in histories of the subject. The problem is, however, that some of these 'striking' traits may have been described too simply and categorically as workings of a 'political-' or 'command economy.' Leaving aside the huge operation of empire-wide tax collection and the state-subsidised corn supply of Rome itself, the *annona*,[5] let us instead focus on some topics more relevant to this study.

The default position on redistribution in Roman Britain is that this was exercised primarily through the provincial government and the army. To deal with the former first, it is a question of the interaction between the collection of taxes from the rural inhabitants of the countryside and the development of cities and urban markets: Collingwood argued that towns were 'parasitic and essentially a thing of luxury,' but that they had important political and cultural functions,[6] which is a claim also propounded by Finley about the cities of antiquity in general,[7] whilst nearly every other major work on the history of Roman

---

[1] K. Polanyi and C. Arensberg, 'Preface,' in K. Polanyi, C. Arensberg and H. W. Pearson (eds), *Trade and Market in the Early Empires* (Glencoe, IL; 1957), p. viii.
[2] Polanyi, 'The Economy as Instituted Process,' p. 253; cf. Douglas North's parallel argument about 'formal institutional constraints' which result in particular exchange organisations: D. North, *Institutions, Institutional Change and Economic Performance* (Cambridge, 1990), p. 47.
[3] Polanyi, 'The Economy as Instituted Process,' p. 256.
[4] Polanyi, 'The Economy as Instituted Process,' p. 256.
[5] A recent work on the subject is P. Erdkamp, *The Grain Market in the Roman Empire: A Social, Political and Economic Study* (Cambridge, 2005).
[6] Collingwood, *Roman Britain*, pp. 198–99.
[7] Finley, *The Ancient Economy*, p. 125.

Britain has claimed that to some extent there was a symbiosis of city and countryside which had greatly beneficent economic effects on the occupants of the rural areas.[8]

Secondly, there is the question of the army as an institutional, state-financed producer and consumer of goods on a large scale. The Roman army excelled in all kinds of building projects, civilian as well as military, and at different times and in different places it also acted as a producer of pottery, tiles, tools and weapons, leather, timber and metals—all for its own purposes.[9] It may well be, however, that it was as a consumer that the army had the greatest impact on civilian society, for it is believed that official arrangements, large-scale contracts, were employed to meet its basic requirements for food and materials. If this is true, very large manufacturers could have thrived on supplying the military market exempt from normal commercial considerations: the army could obtain the necessary goods at exceptionally low prices, and the producers could have been guaranteed that everything produced would be sold at the agreed price.[10] Furthermore, there is the question of how imports of substantial shipments of Mediterranean commodities like olive oil, wine, fish-sauce and spices found their way to Britain, which we will return to in chapter six.

In the following, we will be enquiring into the workings of the local command economy of Vindolanda: did the material demands of the army and the requirements of its own manufacturing activity stimulate civilian production of either finished goods or raw materials?[11] Moreover, was grain for the army purchased at set prices and did this practice encourage a significant growth of agricultural production?[12] Or did it just cause farmers to produce that extra amount, tantamount to a sort of added indirect taxation, without their turning to the farming of cash crops?[13]

In short, the primary question becomes whether or not tax-collection and the necessary channelling of corn and supplies to the army stifled or stimulated the economy of the province. Also, how was the social structure of the command economy constituted? If the Vindolanda Tablets can shed some light on either of these two overall questions, we might just become a little wiser on the role of redistribution in the ancient economy.

Three case studies
Tab.Vindol. II.**155**, in translation:

> 25th April, at service, 343 men.
> of these: shoemakers ... 12.
> builders to the bathhouse, 18.
> for lead ...
> for ... wagons (?)
> ... hospital ...
> to the kilns ...
> for clay ...
> plasterers ...
> for ... tents (?) ...
> for rubble ...
> ...[14]

This short and, sadly, fragmented list of men engaged in work and their professions belongs to the occupancy of the 9th Cohort of Batavians in *c.* AD 97/100–05, when the garrison of Vindolanda numbered probably just over a thousand men.[15] Therefore, it is quite interesting to learn that more than a third of the military establishments' nominal strength could routinely be detailed to ordinary work duties. Much of it seems to be related to either construction activity or connected with it (plausibly, work on the fort in this period required a lot of manpower and materials), but we also see mention of shoemakers and men for something to do with tents. A couple of similar tablets confirm the overall picture, whilst one seems to be dealing with military equipment specifically.[16]

Moreover, comparable lists of men detailed for work duties survive from *Dura-Europus* and Bu Njem: at the former, the dispatch of soldiers for procuring barley, arranging for its transportation or escort, fetching wood and dispatched on various errands as messengers and carriers of letters is recorded; at the latter, daily reports of the doings of the garrison attest to, among other things, men fetching water for the baths, gathering wood, attending camels and donkeys, exercising craftsmanship and doing construction work (although only on a minor scale), feeding the furnace at the bathhouse as well as the oven at the bakery, and acting as messengers in various contexts.[17]

In fact, a multitude of different letters shed a diffuse light on some of the infrastructural improvements made by the

---

[8] Rivet, *Town and Country*, p. 126; Frere, *Britannia*, p. 254; Wacher, *Roman Britain*, pp. 88, 107; and Salway, *Roman Britain*, pp. 235–38, 619–25.
[9] See, for instance, Frere, *Britannia*, pp. 215–17.
[10] See Salway, *Roman Britain*, pp. 650–51.
[11] Cf. Richmond, *Roman Britain*, pp. 132–33; and Frere, *Britannia*, pp. 215–16, 281.
[12] Cf. Frere, *Britannia*, pp. 217, 260, 265; Wacher, *Roman Britain*, p. 141; and M. Todd, *Roman Britain* (London, 1999), p. 110.
[13] Cf. Collingwood, *Roman Britain*, p. 226; Rivet, *Town and Country*, p. 122; and Wacher, *Roman Britain*, p. 106.
[14] *Tab.Vindol.* II, p. 99; with amendment in l. 1 from *Tab.Vindol.* III, p. 155.
[15] A. R. Birley, *Garrison Life*, p. 62.
[16] *Tab.Vindol.* II.156, 157, 160.
[17] Cf. *P.Dura-Europus* 82, col. ii; and *O.bu.njem.* 1–62.

Roman forces garrisoning the frontier. For instance, tablets from Vindolanda reveal the routine nature of transport: roads (and bridges)[18] were in place and carts and draught animals were available to ship consignments of quarried stone or grain about.[19] On the same note, the frontier forces guarded roads and key nodes in the transportation network: at *Mons Claudianus* several *ostraca* reveal how 'road sentinels' were instructed to aid travellers, and local soldiers were dispatched to accompany travellers and provide them with escort- and guide services.[20] At this combined desert garrison and mining station, moreover, the miners often reported directly to the prefect in charge, and not, significantly, to the civilian officials overseeing the work in the quarries.[21] Finally, the army's expertise in the construction and development of systems of steady water supply must have been a boon to soldiers and local civilians alike: especially in a torrid place like the Egyptian desert—were well-preserved letters reveal the garrison's ever-present worries over water—but also in more temperate climates like that of *Vindonissa*.[22]

The implication is, therefore, that there was a lot of economic activity going on in the guise of 'military work,' for although it is obvious that military units carry out some degree of basic supply and maintenance operations themselves, this fact by no means takes away from the economic significance of up to one third of the Roman army on the northern frontier (if we extrapolate from the figures attested at Vindolanda) being engaged in some kind of productive labour;[23] furthermore, shoemakers and similar craftsmen would have required processed materials for their work, whilst artisans and construction workers were reliant on the availability of both processed and raw materials in large quantities, thus stimulating the production of suppliers or 'sub-contractors.'[24]

In short, this kind of workforce and, not least, the size of it, must have created a demand that had to be satisfied by either the specific garrison itself, other military units, civilians, or by specialised contractors; and through mining, processing and building, the military garrisons would have developed the infrastructure of their own hinterlands. All of these activities can certainly be labelled 'economic,' and as they were the result of work done by soldiers, paid for with money raised through taxes, we see the working and consequences of redistribution on an empire-wide scale: taxes raised in various provinces, and mainly in the rich, peaceful ones, were expended on the army and its activities in less profitable (or, as was probably sometimes the case, loss-making) frontier provinces. Indeed, even the actual process of paying the troops is attested by a fragmented tablet from *Vindolanda* which may concern the payment of a century, while a strength report from *Dura-Europus* records the coming and going of men sent to arrange for the payments of the entire garrison.[25]

Lastly, it should not be forgotten that the presence of the army and, more significantly, its policing operations must have had a major stabilising effect on areas which had hitherto seen a fair amount of conflict and which had lacked laws guaranteeing protection of life and goods. Thus, we find that the cohorts stationed at *Vindolanda* were spread out to quite a considerable degree with contingents of soldiers dispatched near and far on various errands and units assigned to individual local duty stations.[26] The same state of affairs is even more evident at *Dura-Europus*,[27] while travellers going to or from *Mons Claudianus* had to obtain 'right of passage'-documents in order to be allowed through military checkpoints,[28] and at *Vindonissa* soldiers patrolled the streets of nearby settlements[29]—accordingly, it is fair to say that the prosperity of the *Pax Romana* was a result of this huge, concerted peacekeeping operation.

However, to round off this discussion of the local infrastructural and economic benefits of the Vindolandan garrison, it would be highly interesting to examine how self-sufficient this military command economy borne out of an imperial, political economy really was. Did the Roman army satisfy all of its demands through its own huge supply operation, or did it combine the requirements of a command economy with the more risky, but less expensive, supply of goods to be obtained through the 'free' civilian market? Let us turn to another tablet to try and answer these questions.

Tab.Vindol. II.**180**, in translation:

> Account of wheat measured out from that which
> I myself have put into the barrel:
> to myself, for bread ...
> to Macrinus, *modii* 7.
> to Felicius Victor on the order of Spectatus
> provided as a loan (?), *modii* 26.
> in three sacks, to father, *modii* 19.
> to Macrinus, *modii* 13.
> to the ox herds at the wood, *modii* 8.

---

[18] *Tab.Vindol.* II.258 may concern the construction of a bridge.
[19] *Tab.Vindol.* II.314–16, III.583–85, 649.
[20] *O.claud.* II.357–59, 374; IV.889.
[21] *O.claud.* IV.850, 862, 868.
[22] *O.claud.* I.2, II.362, 380; *Tab.Vindon.* 4.
[23] A. R. Birley, *Garrison Life*, deals with some of the archaeological evidence of 'industrial activity,' as he calls it, pp. 56, 65, 69. More recently, though, increasing evidence of production and manufacture at Vindolanda has been accumulated—in particular, a magnetometer survey to the north of the fort has indicated a sprawling layout of sites probably related to production activity; see Birley and Blake, *The Excavations of 2005–2006*, pp. 1–3, 72.
[24] The tablets also attest the presence at Vindolanda of shield-makers, brewers, bath-men, veterinarians, carpenters, maltsters and pharmacists, to mention some of the more significant trades; see Appendix.
[25] *Tab.Vindol.* II.242; *P.Dura-Europus* 95, col. i.29–col. ii.8.; moreover, *Tab.Vindon.* 4 (see above, p. 21) constitutes a 'paycheck.'
[26] Cf. *Tab.Vindol.* II.154, III.575, 628 in particular, but also *Tab.Vindol.* II.127–53, III.574, 576–79.
[27] *P.Dura-Europus* 100–03, 107–10.
[28] *O.Claud.* I.48–82, II.363.
[29] *Tab.Vindon.* 30.

likewise to Amabilis at the shrine, *modii* 3.
6–11th (?) September, to Crescens
on the order of Firmus (?), *modii* 3.
likewise ..., *modii* ...
to Macr... ..., *modii* (?) 15.
likewise to Ma... (?), *modii* ...
to father ..., *modii* 2.
26th September.
to Lu... the *beneficiarius*, *modii* 6.
to Felicius Victor, *modii* 15.
for twisted loaves (?), to you, *modii* 2.
to Crescens, *modii* 9.
to the legionary soldiers on the order of Firmus, *modii* 11+
to Candidus, *modii* ...
to you, in a sack from Briga (?), ...
to you, ...
to Lucco, in charge of the pigs ...
to Primus, slave (?) of Lucius ...
to you ...
to Lucco for his own use ...
likewise that which I have sent ... *modii* ... (?)
in the century of Voturius (?)
to father, in charge of the oxen ...
likewise, within the measure ... (?)
15 pounds yield 15+ pounds (?) ...
total, *modii* ...
likewise to myself, for bread, *modii* ...
total of wheat, *modii* 320½.[30]

This account of the disbursement of wheat[31] is highly interesting in itself, but what makes it truly significant is the fact that it was written by the same hand as tablets **181** (an account of various commodities sold) and **344** (the letter of complaint written by an 'overseas man,' quoted above, p. 18).[32] Accordingly, we have evidence of a trader, a civilian, who was in charge of distributing grain to various members of the military garrison and who seems to have provided the grain himself.

First of all, this is quite a large amount of grain: employing the same figure of one seventh *modius* of wheat per man per day (as in the treatment of tablet **343**) for an active man fed on bread alone, this amount of 320½ *modii* would provide 2,240 daily rations.[33] We do not know how much time the account covered, but there are two references to the month of September, maybe indicating that it was no more than a month or so.

The people listed as recipients range from a possible slave, oxherds, a swineherd, a possible priest, a *beneficiarius*, legionaries and single names which probably denote ordinary members of the auxiliary cohort. Of further interest is the fact that a Spectatus and a Firmus, who are likely to be the persons named in Octavius' letter as well, ordered the distribution of grain; that one person, Felicius Victor, received his allotment as a loan; and that the 'overseas trader' in charge of the account disbursed grain to himself twice, 'to you' four times, and twice 'to father.'

Although it is impossible to ascertain the exact nature of the account, it does provide a lot of information in itself as to what it is and what it is not: it is a private account written for the benefit of two persons who were on very familiar terms (implied by the use of 'myself,' 'you' and the reference to 'father'); this private nature of the account also seems to indicate that the 'overseas trader' was acting in a civilian capacity and needed to keep an account only for himself and an associate; however, although the distribution was managed in a private capacity, it was also a controlled supply process, for disbursements could be ordered and people obtained allotments in different personal capacities (contrast 'to Lucco, in charge of the pigs' with 'to Lucco, for his own use'); lastly, it was not based on individual payment and there are no concrete hints that it had anything to do with an official military supply system.

Finally, it is necessary to consider briefly some issues inherent in this arrangement, but which we cannot settle decisively: on the one hand, the provenance of this not inconsiderable quantity of wheat is unknown, although we do know that the author of the account 'measured it out from that which he himself put into the barrel,'[34] that he was a trader who dealt in various commodities (tablet **181**), that we may have another reference to grain (tablet **344**, see above p. 18: something about 'goods' being 'poured down the drain'), and that we know of the entrepreneurial activities of the contemporary Octavius in buying up more than fifteen times as much wheat (tablet **343**); on the other hand, although the exact transactional relationship between entrepreneur and army is also unattested, we can tell that no money changed hands and that only one person was being put down as a debtor, while relations of the author received disbursements on a par with military personnel.

To sum up, tablet **180** taken in conjunction with tablets **181** and **344** provides testimony of a civilian entrepreneur not only trading with the Roman army, but actually being entrusted with part of the military food supply, as well.

---

[30] *Tab.Vindol.* II, p. 123.
[31] The Latin simply reads *ratio frumenti*, so the exact nature of the wheat is unknown (*Tab.Vindol.* II.180, l. 1).
[32] Furthermore, as tablet **180** was found together with tablet **343** (Octavius' letter to Candidus), the Candidus mentioned in both tablets might be the same person.
[33] Some misleading figures have found their way into wider circulation. Whittaker, 'Supplying the Army,' pp. 204–34, says of *Tab.Vindol.* II.180 on p. 213, for example, that 'the recorded total is substantial—2,000 *modii* issued over ten days of September, which would have been enough to feed 200 people.' The data actually implies a somewhat different reading. Firstly, the recorded total is 320½ *modii* and not 2000; second, only some of the entries record disbursements between a date that falls within 6–11th September (we can only infer that it is '<(*ante diem*)> [...]. *Idus Septem(bres),*' see l. 11) and 26th September (that is '<(*ante diem*)> vi *Kal(endas)* [*O*]*ctobr[es],*' see l. 17), and as these two are the only days attested, it is misleading to suggest that the wheat was issued over ten days of September; and lastly, 320½ *modii* would feed 200 men for ten (possibly eleven) days. It follows that 2000 *modii*, if that had been the figure, would have fed 200 men for seventy days or 1,400 men for ten days.
[34] *Tab.Vindol.* II.180, ll. 1–2: *ratio frumenti em[ensi ex quo] ipse dedi in cupam.*

Based on the evidence of tablet **344** and **180** for the author's civilian status, and the fact that disbursements could be ordered, it certainly appears difficult to argue that the account was not written by a civilian in military employ, but that the list was comprised by a military quartermaster as part of his professional duties.

Rather on the contrary, the formal character of surviving military records highlights the difference in nature between the account kept by the author of tablet **180** and official accounts written for professional purposes: at both Vindolanda, Bu Njem and *Mons Claudianus*, for instance, various letters and records relating to food supply leave little doubt about either the military nature of the supply itself or about the military status of the involved personnel.[35] More significantly, however, a letter from *Dura-Europus* provides testimony of a freedman administering supplies of barley from imperial estates to military personnel—and even denying a very senior officer provisions for some of his men.[36] Thus, although we should not confuse civilian agents with soldiers, neither should we distinguish too rigidly between civilian and military food supply when, in fact, these two spheres of activity often seem to have overlapped.[37]

Moreover, it may be possible to infer that the grain was obtained privately, outside the sphere and influence of any command economy, and then distributed over a period of time by the same civilian entrepreneur according to some contractual agreement entered into between the author of the account and the relevant military officials at *Vindolanda*—by analogy a sort of military 'outsourcing' of part of the overall supply operation. The opposite process, of goods obtained by the military through redistributive channels but put up for sale on the local market, also seems to be attested by the activities of Cassius Saecularis in collaboration with friends and colleagues (treated above, p. 22).[38]

Accordingly, this tablet suggests that the extent and dominance of 'command economies' in the Roman Empire in general, and in the frontier zones in particular, should be reconsidered. For although this kind of economic relationship is still to be considered as redistributive, it intersects with the 'free economy' at a very early point and thereby employs different channels and mechanisms than has hitherto been envisaged in traditional studies of Roman army supply. Moreover, while military contracts do reflect redistributive processes, it is important to keep in mind that these contracts still had to be settled under some sort of market conditions. Thus, this kind of 'micro-contracting' has little to do with economic models where the entire economy of the Roman Empire was simply, in effect, a redistributive machine collecting money for the emperor, who could then set in motion huge state-financed supply operations to sustain legions guarding distant frontiers.[39]

Tab.Luguval. **16**, in translation:

> Docilis to Augurinus his prefect, greetings. As you ordered, we have attached below all the names of lancers who were missing lances, either who did not have fighting lances, or who (did not have) the smaller *subarmales*, or who (did not have) regulation swords. Troop of Genialis senior: Verecundus, (one) fighting lance and two *subarmales*. Troop of Albinus [*whole page lost*. Troop of *name*]: Docca, two *subarmales*. Troop of Docilis: Pastor, two *subarmales*; Felicio, (one) fighting lance. Troop of Sollemnis: [...]atus, (one) fighting lance and two *subarmales*. Troop of Mansuetus: [...]s, (one) fighting lance; Victorinus (?) son of [...]ra, (one) fighting lance. Troop of Martialis: [...]so, (one) fighting lance. Troop of Genialis: Festus, two *subarmales*; Maior, two *subarmales*; [*name*], [two] *subarmales*; [*name*] (one) fighting lance. Troop of Victor: [...]. (*2nd hand*) May you fare well, Augurinus, with your family, (my) lord.[40]

Although this text is drawn from the Carlisle Tablets there are no immediate problems in comparing its contents with those of the Vindolanda Tablets: indeed, *Luguvalium*, that is modern day Carlisle, lay only some forty kilometres west of Vindolanda and was part of the same early Tyne-Solway frontier, the Stanegate Road;[41] in addition, the tablets are reckoned to be from the period *c.* AD 79–125 and are therefore contemporary with their Vindolandan counterparts.[42]

Like the first of the three case studies this text comprises a military account, but unlike tablet **155**, which seemed to be for the personal reference of a scribe only, this one has all the trappings of an official document. The contrast becomes even more marked if one compares this official petition for supply of weapons with two instances of civilians supplying vital necessities: **180**, an account of wheat supplied, and **861**, an account of, particularly, spears sold to soldiers. Accordingly, it is tempting to claim that whereas *Tab.Luguval.* **16** represents the workings of a command economy proper, *Tab.Vindol.* **180** and **861** represent the fusion of command economy and free market. We will return to this economic dichotomy evident in the supply system later.

The most important point to be made about the information contained in this account of cavalrymen

---

[35] Cf. *Tab.Vindol.* II.159, III.583–85; *O.Bu.Njem* 72, 76–81, 94–95; *O.Claud.* I.148–49. Most of these to be treated below, pp. 30–31.
[36] *P.Dura-Europus* 64.A.
[37] Cf. Whittaker, *Frontiers*, 207.
[38] Cf. *Tab.Vindol.* II.213, 215.
[39] For a discussion of authors proposing a more rigid, structural, political economy, see chapter six on Erdkamp and Monfort.
[40] Tomlin, 'Roman Manuscripts from Carlisle,' p. 57.
[41] See map, chapter six, p. 46.
[42] Tomlin, 'Roman Manuscripts from Carlisle,' p. 32.

missing their weapons is maybe also the most obvious one: it speaks of a very organised system of supply and replenishment, where the loss of three different kinds of regulation weapons seems to be of no great concern, because, by implication, they could be supplied without too much trouble. In fact, it is notable that the cavalry commander had only to write a thorough and, apparently, completely routine list of who was missing what, and that he did so 'as ordered' by his prefect.[43] Furthermore, surviving documents reveal that cavalry mounts were routinely distributed in much the same way at *Dura-Europus*: individual cavalrymen were assigned specific horses, each carefully identified by its primary characteristics, and most of them with a recorded value of 125 *denarii*—implying some kind of fixed price for new purchases.[44]

In consequence, taking into consideration that Vindolanda and *Luguvalium* were part of the same defensive line, we must also assume that they were part of the same military supply system, the same command economy in other words. Hence, both the two kinds of economic activity attested in the above, one based on handing over supply to a contractor and one based on the formal hierarchy and supply apparatus of the army itself, must have been present all along the Tyne-Solway frontier—at the very least.

Moreover, these three case studies represent a mere sample of the evidence that exists in the tablets to support this inference, and it is on this entire *corpus* of material that the following section draws.[45]

Conclusions drawn from miscellaneous tablets
Although the basic principle of this kind of economic activity is the redistribution of means by the state, it appears that direct involvement of an official supply apparatus was not as prominent in this kind of economic behaviour as is otherwise often assumed. This is not to say that food, equipment and salaries were not obtained using money raised through taxes, but rather, it is to say that redistributive channels relied increasingly on the market as a go-between exchanging taxes in kind for cash and cash for specific supplies needed. Indeed, the only concrete piece of evidence for redistribution in a traditional sense is an account headed 'revenues of the fort,' *reditus castelli*, listing daily incomes (apparently around 32 *denarii* per day) over five days of July, which may possibly illustrate this process of exchanging taxes or customs levied in kind for cash.[46]

However, this argument does not conform well with one of the most important works on the subject in recent times, which states that 'no prudent emperor could leave the supply of the army up to chance, and certainly not to the hazards of whether traders and the market thought it worthwhile to take up such contracts.'[47] Though this seems to be a logical, common sense argument, it tends to assume the dominance of a 'traditional' command economy behaviour which is not really to be found in the Vindolanda Tablets, where, on the contrary, we come across a surprising amount of evidence that points to the role and importance of non-military economic activity.

First of all, however, let us contrast the evidence for civilians supplying the army with what is presumed to be the official food supply for a 500-strong cavalry regiment, a quingenary *ala*, based in Carlisle:

Troop of Genialis:
    42 bushels of barley.
    18 bushels of wheat.
Troop of Agilis:
    39 bushels of barley.
    18 bushels of wheat.
[*13 similar preserved entries follow, then at the end of the document:*]
Total bushels of barley: 669.
bushels of wheat: 267.[48]

This account is a lot more in keeping with the traditional view on military supply, and in its basic composition it is very similar to the other Carlisle Tablet treated in the above. It is assumed to be concerned with the distribution of three days' worth of rations to the regiment, with the barley being used as feed for the horses and the wheat to make bread for the men.

Likewise, a highly fragmented tablet from *Vindolanda* seems to be concerned with barley for a cavalry detachment, a *turma*,[49] and while official accounts of barley stored and new wagon-loads received have also survived,[50] it is, however, tablet **649** which provides the most tantalising glimpse: local natives are carting around 381 *modii* of emmer wheat, *bracis*, and either they or others doing transport duty in relation to *Vindolanda* are paid in cash for their services according to established custom[51]—hence, this tablet plausibly concerns the collection and freight of tax grain, possibly by civilian contractors, but unfortunately the fragmented narrative

---

[43] Tab.Luguval. 16, l. 3: *ita ut praecepisti*.
[44] *P.Dura-Europus* 56, 97.
[45] See Appendix.
[46] *Tab.Vindol.* II.178.
[47] Whittaker, *Frontiers*, p. 110.
[48] *Tab.Luguval.* 1A, p. 44; although the author of the article has chosen to translate the measure of volume as 'bushels,' the original measure used in the Latin is still *modii* and therefore directly comparable to *Tab.Vindol.* II.180.
[49] *Tab.Vindol.* I.159.
[50] *Tab.Vindol.* III.583–85.
[51] That is, the wagon-drivers are paid *vectura* (fee for transport of goods) and *velatura* (payment for contracting), see discussion in E. Birley *et al.*, *The Early Wooden Forts: Reports*, p. 29; *vectura* is also paid in *Tab.Vindol.* III.615.

provides no decisive clues.⁵²

Moreover, an *ostracon* from Bu Njem records the arrival of a caravan of mules and donkeys carrying barley, and there are numerous messages about wheat shipped back to the fort by civilian caravans, while military purveyors of grain, *frumentarii*, are mentioned in other contexts.⁵³ Finally, *papyri* from *Dura-Europus* reveal how soldiers were allocated money (the receipt of which they had to acknowledge in writing) in order that they be sent on official errands to purchase barley.⁵⁴ Accordingly, a number of sources illustrate the workings of the command economy proper. Food supply could, therefore, equally well be in the hands of either soldiers or civilians.

However, army officials accounting for the way they obtained supplies also attest to the way that the military economy intersected with the free trading sector in a number of ways. For instance, tablet **185** seems to comprise a list of travel expenses incurred either during a long stay at the military establishment of *Isurium* (Aldborough), north of the legionary fortress of *Eburacum* (York), and going back to Vindolanda, or during a trip from Vindolanda to *Eburacum* and back again.⁵⁵ In a seemingly haphazard manner the list accounts for either the date or the place where expenses were incurred, and the commodities purchased range from a lot of cheap wine, salt, fodder, and two wagon-axles for a carriage to accommodation and vests. At the end, the account has a 'total' of 78¾ *denarii* and a 'grand total' of 94¾ *denarii*, which adds further significance to the alleged purpose of writing such a list of expenses: if this was an account of personal expenses, would there really be a need for such a meticulous list? It is more likely, on the whole, that this is a list of travel expenses recorded with the aim of eventual reimbursement at Vindolanda. If that is the way of it, tablet **185** represents another aspect of the military economy with the state coffers having payed for somebody's official trip—and it is echoed by the mention of a 'travel allowance,' *viaticum*, in two other fragments.⁵⁶

For present purposes, however, the significance of this list of expenses is that we witness, once again, how the military economy relied not on command or actual physical redistribution, but on another economic sphere where the relevant demands could be satisfied by the ready use of cash: even an officer travelling between military stations had to pay for accommodation and barley for his horses. There is no hint of military requisition or an internal mechanism of supply within the army as a closed economic system.

This draws our attention to a wider issue: the scope of the command economy in the sense of what it could and could not provide on its own, and the extent to which it was integrated economically with its hinterland and the province in general—just consider how tablet **343** (Octavius' letter to Candidus) revealed a considerable network of people engaged in various kinds of commerce, and similar tablets (like **642,** quoted above, p. 1; and **648**) lend further credibility to the existence of loose, civilian groupings exchanging services and commodities.

However, the evidence we have for some sort of fort-hinterland interaction is ambiguous and therefore also highly interesting: on the one hand, we have an account like that of tablet **186** which appears to be concerned with the official purchase of supplies through middlemen (who could be slaves, soldiers or civilians), whilst tablets **604** and **607** comprise two dated accounts of the purchase of goods necessary for repairs, which are then listed below. The thing is, though, that in the case of tablet **186** the supplies which apparently had to be bought in from outside, through middlemen, were commodities like salt, Celtic beer, possibly goat-meat and pork, while 100 boot nails were sold to one of these middlemen; and tablets **604** and **607**, these two written by the same hand, record the purchase of 350 boot nails and a length of yarn, respectively, so that the shoes and clothes of named soldiers could be repaired.⁵⁷

On the other hand, and in marked contrast, tablets **309**, **314-316** and **628** attest, in the named order, a carpenter, who appears to have been in military employ, dispatching a great quantity of pre-fabricated wooden objects (like axles and spokes) as supplies free of charge; the routine business of carting supplies of lime and quarried stone about, as well as the allocation of transport in general; and a *decurion*, that is, an officer of a troop of cavalry, routinely requesting beer to be sent to him and his men (hence, the name of this chapter), who were not half a day's travel from Vindolanda—the latter tablet being mirrored by a fragment from *Vindonissa* in which nail-studded sandals are ordered from the fort, so that the sender and his men could be on the march as soon as possible.⁵⁸

Moreover, as concerns the work done in military workshops, tablet **597** accounts for simple repairs made to an odd miscellany of items, while **598** and **600** are lists of equipment for wagons (probably denoting objects manufactured). Finally, the recently published tablet **862** constitutes a routine record of the daily work done by a *fabrica*, the skilled craftsmen of a century: once again we find spare parts for wagons being produced, and in addition basic metalworking was being undertaken.

To sum up, there seems to have been some narrow limits to the extent of the command economy, both as to the scope of commodities that it could provide from within

---

⁵² *Tab.Vindol.* III.649—it is even possible that the letter pertains to business between civilian partners, like that of Octavius and Candidus (*Tab.Vindol.* I.343) or Maior and Maritimus (*Tab.Vindol.* III.645).
⁵³ *O.Bu.Njem* 72, 76–81, 94–95.
⁵⁴ *P.Dura-Europus* 129.
⁵⁵ See map, chapter six, p. 46.
⁵⁶ *Tab.Vindol.* II.283, 330. In contrast, *P.Dura-Europus* 60B is a letter ordering military units to record expenses incurred due to hosting a Parthian envoy and report them back to the governor.
⁵⁷ *Tab. Vindol.* III.603 and 605 are also accounts of nails used.
⁵⁸ *Tab. Vindol.* II.309, 314–16, III.628; *Tab.Vindon.* 36.

itself and as to a coordinated use of the institution of the market. For one would ordinarily expect that the Roman army could supply its own troops with basic necessities like salt, beer and pork, and certainly with something as commonplace as boot nails and yarn! At the same time, it is quite surprising that in one instance we see an official selling boot nails to somebody outside the military economy, when, in another instance, we see a craftsman who had to purchase boot nails because none were apparently available (although it is of relevance that tablet **186** dates from Period IV and tablets **604** and **607** from Period III—however, in **601**, likewise from Period III, nails were sold on several different occasions). Furthermore, this has to be contrasted with easy and free supply of carpentry products, transport, beer, spare parts of various kinds, and metalworking.

The overall picture appears rather confusing if one still wishes to perceive of the supply operation of Vindolanda in particular, and the Roman frontier forces in general, as part of one coherent system only. It is possible, though, to hypothesise that *Luguvalium* was a major centre of activity associated with the military headquarters of the entire frontier zone,[59] and that the redistributive apparatus of the Roman army therefore supplied all of its needs, whereas Vindolanda was a less prominent fort which had to obtain goods which never reached it through the official channels in any way it could.

However, two objections can be voiced against this interpretation: first, that Vindolanda was not a backwater fort during the days of the Stanegate frontier which the tablets date from; and secondly, that lack of evidence for private, civilian economic activity at *Luguvalium* and a corresponding lack of attested state influence on matters of supply at Vindolanda cannot support any conclusions,[60] but only serve to highlight the random and fragmented nature of the evidence. Hence, it seems quite impossible to relegate this ambivalence of the sources to different periods of occupation or to some complex, but still rational, system of accounting for the exchange of goods between different branches of the military community—it has to be explained more cautiously as part of the nature of the redistributive system in general.

All in all, the most defining feature of the supply system seems to have been the two-fold way in which it could operate either within the military system alone or make use of middlemen, civilian or not, who could be in the employ of the army, as contractors, or who just had regular commercial dealings with it. The recurrence of some of the names of such middlemen is certainly striking.[61] Furthermore, it seems as if there were no set rules as to what part of the overall supply could be obtained through traders and the market, and what part of the supply it was deemed vital for the Roman army to be in sole control of itself. Normally, food supply and weaponry would be considered such areas of vital importance, but, as we have seen, the supply of grain and spears could be in the hands of entrepreneurs as well as in the hands of the army's own officials.

Concluding remarks on redistribution
Two distinctive modes of economic activity have been plain from the very outset of the analysis conducted in this chapter: on the one hand, we have the supply of the army by itself and from 'within,' that is to say that goods and food were obtained through official channels and distributed by relevant army personnel; on the other hand, we witness a sort of 'outsourced' supply process which entailed that redistribution as a means of satisfying material demand merged with the possibility of obtaining supplies through market exchange, when and where possible.

Therefore, we can conclude that the social structure of the supply system was actually based on two different kinds of organisation: a supply structure manned by military officials from top to bottom, and a parallel structure where military officials at the top supplied money and knowledge of the demand in question, and one or more middlemen or entrepreneurs, who may have been either soldiers or civilians, proceeded to connect that demand with various suppliers who would probably have been local producers in the province itself.

When demand was satisfied through supply channelled by the command economy there is little way of knowing, beyond mere conjecture, whether or not the set prices were enough to stimulate the general production of the province, but when it was satisfied through entrepreneurs acting as middlemen, these must have been forced to obtain their goods through some sort of market situation and, hence, to have incurred a profit amongst both themselves as a commercial class and amongst the native producers of their wares.

However, before drawing this chapter to a close, it should be mentioned explicitly that the Vindolanda Tablets seen in isolation actually provide very little evidence for an empire-wide command economy directing the movements of various goods unobtainable in the northern provinces to Britain, or for any kind of overarching imperial or army organisation whose responsibility it was to administer money and supplies to the army in the various frontier provinces.[62]

In conclusion, as concerns the nature of the economic activity conducted within the framework of the political economy, the primacy of cash and meticulous accounting is once again forcefully attested, stressing the unembedded nature of the transactions. Social obligations can be discerned here and there, but they are very much secondary to more formal economic considerations.

---

[59] As it became after the construction of Hadrian's Wall; see Frere, *Britannia*, p. 122; and Salway, *Roman Britain*, p. 184.
[60] As a matter of fact, there are plenty of official, military documents among the Vindolanda *corpus* (most notably *Tab.Vindol.* II. 127–77; and *Tab.Vindol.* III. 574–80).
[61] For instance, the *homo transmarinus* of *Tab. Vindol.* II.180, 181, 344; 'Gavo' from *Tab. Vindol.* II.192, 207; and 'Gracilis' and 'Audax' in *Tab. Vindol.* II.186.
[62] Unless, of course, the single reference to the *Caesariani* in *Tab.Vindol.* III.645 is to be interpreted as substantial evidence for an empire-wide supply apparatus.

Regarding the scale of the Roman command economy, however, the evidence points towards both instances of highly formal and organised activity as well as cases of underdeveloped, seemingly *ad hoc* supply practices, leaving us with an impression of a more dynamic and flexible command economy than is often otherwise assumed.

Chapter 5
Reciprocity: The 'Social Economy' of a Military Community

Reciprocity and economic embeddedness

Arguably the most unfamiliar category of economic activity to be dealt with in this study is that of reciprocity. 'Unfamiliar' not so much because of the way that the concept is defined, but because it is rarely awarded any kind of significance in traditional economic studies, and because it is rather more difficult to identify embedded economic activity in historical sources than it is to identify either market exchange or redistribution. Indeed, it might just be the case that this kind of 'socially determined' transaction is often missing from the historical record, as these transactions are based mostly upon mutual, oral agreement between one or more individuals, and not upon formal, written contracts codifying transactional relationships between strangers. Although one might therefore expect source material to be biased against this particular dimension of economic activity, it is still possible to glean a certain amount of positive evidence for its existence from the Vindolanda Tablets.

First of all, Polanyi's basic tenet was that in so far as social practices are intertwined with both the production and transportation of goods, as well as the acts of circulating and administering them, we can talk of a process in which social activities are also economic activities; hence, humanly devised institutions which govern social practices with economic implications are also 'economic' in themselves.[1] Bearing this in mind, 'reciprocity denotes movements between correlative points of symmetrical groupings,'[2] and:

> —voluntary and semi-voluntary associations of a military, vocational, religious or social character create situations in which, at least transitorily or in regard to a given locality or typical situation, there would form symmetrical groupings the members of which practice some sort of mutuality.[3]

'Symmetrical,' in this context, is supposed to be understood as indicating 'similar social arrangements and culture traits.'[4] Accordingly, within a military community where the members were all Germanic auxiliaries resident at Vindolanda, and therefore socially and culturally 'symmetrical,' groupings would form, for instance within each century or among the officers of the cohort, the members of which would then 'practice some sort of mutuality'—exchange based on reciprocity. Specific transactions aside, just consider the strong ties evident in the closing passage of a letter written by a soldier absent on leave to his comrade back at the fort of *Vindonissa*: 'And also in order that you may write back to me from the cohort, so that you always keep in mind to write me back in reply.'[5]

In particular, economic reciprocity could be in the guise of soldiers of the same sub-unit sharing food or equipment with one another as an act of good comradeship, or it could take the form of centurions entertaining one another and reinforcing bonds of cultural significance that marked them out as Romans of status (by, for instance, the consumption of olives and wine), and finally, we would expect it to be exercised by the prefect of the cohort as master of both his own household, the only sizeable one allowed within the walls of the fort, and supreme commander of the garrison: for means expended by the prefect on both a domestic and communal level are also to be considered acts of social value that tied the military community together.

Furthermore, Polanyi elaborated that 'reciprocity as a form of integration gains greatly in power through its capacity of employing both redistribution and [market] exchange as subordinate methods,' which is evident in, for instance, the redistribution of food or valuables according to the social status of the recipients, or through the use of market exchange at fixed prices to the conscious benefit of one or other of the partners in the transaction.[6]

The use of money might appear incongruous in relation to this kind of economic activity, but this is not necessarily so, for the uses of money are, according to Polanyi, 'payment, standard and exchange,' of which only the latter is intimately related with the existence of markets. Payments are made to discharge obligations conferred upon the payer by various social institutions and not only in connection with transactions, while 'the standard or accounting use of money is the equating of

---

[1] Polanyi, 'The Economy as Instituted Process,' pp. 248–49; cf. Douglas North's parallel argument about 'informal institutional constraints' which result in particular exchange organisations: North, *Institutions*, p. 40.
[2] Polanyi, 'The Economy as Instituted Process,' p. 250.
[3] Polanyi, 'The Economy as Instituted Process,' p. 253.
[4] Polanyi, 'Preface,' p. vii.
[5] *Tab.Vindon.* 40, ll. 3–5.
[6] Polanyi, 'The Economy as Instituted Process,' p. 253.

amounts of different kinds of goods for definite purposes.'[7] These 'purposes' can then be of either a transactional nature or to enable the managing of various goods. As regards the subject of prices, reciprocal equivalencies 'determine the amount that is "adequate" in relation to the symmetrically placed party.'[8] In short, the use of money and the existence of a socially embedded economy are in no way mutually exclusive.

Having now defined the concept of reciprocity, the question then becomes how best to utilise this approach, also known as 'substantivism,' and how to characterise patterns of behaviour which lend themselves to this kind of analysis.[9] On the one hand, models of the ancient economy can proclaim a high degree of embeddedness—where markets exist but are of little importance, redistribution is prominent and factors of status, hierarchy and civic influence dominate the distribution of wealth in society—as Finley did in his *The Ancient Economy*;[10] or they can propound the validity of formal economics for the people of antiquity—and thereby stress the existence of ancient markets alongside the redistributive machinery of the Roman state and the socially determined exchanges within social structures like that of the *cliens-patronus* system[11]—as is implicit in the latest version of Hopkins' model.[12]

The purpose of the present chapter is to investigate reciprocity in the Vindolanda Tablets and to relate what new positive evidence they provide as concerns the question of embeddedness in the ancient economy. In order to do so, transactions which seem to be motivated by social obligations, that is to say, non-economic considerations, will be investigated: what is the role of giver in relation to recipient? What is the social status of the giver and what is the reason for giving? How does the transaction cause the recipient(s) to be indebted to the giver or reflect positively on his position in a given social structure or network? In short, the aim is to describe the interaction between status and economic activity as thoroughly as possible.

Three case studies
Tab.Vindol. II.**190**, in translation:

    (b) ... *modii* 3 (?), *denarii* ½.
    ... *denarii* ½.
    (c) ... for the festival, *denarii* ...
    ... for the festival, *denarii* ...
    ... for the festival ...

19th June
of barley ...
of Celtic beer ...
20th June
of barley, *modii* 4+(?).
of Celtic beer, *modii* 2.
21st June, of barley ...
... to the granary (?) ...
...
... *modii* 2.
22nd June
of barley, *modii* 5½ (?).
Allatus (?), of Massic wine (?) ...
23rd June
of barley, *modii* 5½.
of wine, *modius* 1 *sextarii* 14.
of Celtic beer, *modii* 3.
24th June
of barley, *modii* 6+...
of Celtic beer, *modii* 3 *sextarii* ...
of wine, *modius* 1 *sextarii* 12.
of sour wine, *sextarii* 2,
through Privatus.
of fish-sauce, *sextarii* 1½,
through Privatus.
of pork-fat, *sextarii* 10 as a loan (?)
to the lord for charitable donations,
through Privatus.
of wine, *modius* 1 for the festival
of the goddess (?).
of wine, *sextarii* 12,
through Privatus.
25th June
of barley, *sextarii* 11½ (?).
the lords have remained at Briga.[13]

This tablet is thought to have belonged to the household of Flavius Cerialis, prefect of the 9th Cohort of Batavians, who resided at Vindolanda *c.* AD 97/100–05 (Period III). The list itself gives no explicit clues to its own function, but judging from its contents it seems likely that it is some sort of 'domestic account.' It concerns a length of time of approximately one week, from prior to 19th June to the 25th June, and whereas the first part of the account, which is almost completely lost, appears to list commodities, quantities and prices as well as expenses *ad sacrum*,[14] the latter part of it consists entirely of commodities and their respective amounts. It might therefore be suggested that while the fragmented and lost first half of the account concerns expenses in

---

[7] Polanyi, 'The Economy as Instituted Process,' pp. 264–65.
[8] Polanyi, 'The Economy as Instituted Process,' p. 269.
[9] Cf. T. K. Hopkins, 'Sociology and the Substantive View of The Economy,' in K. Polanyi, C. Arensberg and H. W. Pearson (eds), *Trade and Market in the Early Empires* (Glencoe, IL; 1957), p. 299.
[10] Finley, *The Ancient Economy*, in particular chapter two, 'Orders and Status.' For an author on Roman Britain who includes a substantivist perspective, see Millett, *The Romanization of Britain*, pp. 34, 38, 124–26.
[11] *OCD*, s.v. '*patronus*:' 'at Rome, was a man who gave assistance and protection to another person, Roman or non-Roman, who thereby became his client. In return clients gave their patrons respect, deference and services, which included personal attendance and political support.'
[12] Hopkins, 'Rome, Taxes, Rents and Trade,' pp. 190–230.
[13] *Tab.Vindol.* II, p. 153.
[14] *Tab.Vindol.* II.190, ll. c.1–3.

general, the second and preserved half of the list concerns items disbursed or consumed.

The context within which it must be interpreted is that of the *praetorium*, that is, the prefect's household, which although an integrated part of any Roman fort, an official and military place, at the same time doubled as a unique social space where the private sphere of Roman aristocratic life[15] mingled with the public and official duties of a commanding officer. It was neither a secluded island of civilian domesticity surrounded by a sea of savageness, nor simply the private, physical seat of power for the highest ranking officer—it must, quite simply, have been both, like the court of a petty king.

Specifically, the social politics of status, influence and power are attested by a wide range of tablets ranging from officers' families inviting one another to birthday celebrations and holidaying together,[16] via prefects' wives plotting to achieve their own personal—but sadly unknown—ends,[17] to much more serious career-jockeying. For instance, an otherwise unknown colleague petitioned Cerialis to exercise his influence in helping promote the career of a protégé,[18] and two other tablets reveal, on the one hand, Cerialis himself trying to obtain favour with the governor through a high-ranking acquaintance, and, on the other hand, two of his own friends currying favour with him prior to a scheduled appointment with the governor.[19] Thus, the double-sided relationship between the social sphere of life and the politics of command is important for our purposes as it allows us to investigate the link between status and economic behaviour.[20]

First of all, it is of interest that the prefect supplied or donated commodities for a religious festival and particularly that these 'gifts' were quantified and recorded as expenses.[21] These transactions are to be considered under the heading of reciprocity because the supplier had a social responsibility towards the military community with regard to its religious needs: that is, this act of reciprocity was conducted according to the rules of the dual and intertwined relationship between the prefect as patron of the cohort, and the prefect as a wealthy individual responsible for the maintenance of cultic activities. Donations *ad sacrum* can therefore readily be labelled as embedded transactions as they were motivated and regulated by non-economic factors, but since they were recorded as cash sum expenditures, we should also be aware that they were considered to be economic activities—that it mattered whether wine was just consumed as part of the ordinary *praetorium* diet, or was expended as a religious and charitable donation.

The same thing applies to the reference to 'pork-fat as a loan for charitable donations'[22] and 'wine, *modius* 1, for the festival of the goddess (?):'[23] the social status of the prefect implied economic obligations in relation to both the communal and religious spheres of military life. If the normative social circumstances demanded it, then Cerialis had to obtain pork-fat from somewhere (in this case by employing a household slave as an intermediary) so that the expectations could be met. Furthermore, this transaction branches off from another embedded transaction, for Cerialis' slave had obtained the commodity as a loan which was based on the specific relationship between prefect and (unknown) supplier.

We can presume that the rest of the commodities mentioned in the list were disbursements within the *praetorium*: barley for the horses, Celtic beer, wine, sour-wine and fish-sauce for the various members of the staff whom it was the prefect's responsibility as head of the household to keep fed—although it does seem as if 24th June was a day where extra commodities were disbursed and consumed in connection with a religious event: 'the festival of the goddess.' In light of the fact that there was a major festival for *Fors Fortuna* on this day, we may presume that she was, indeed, the goddess in question.[24]

In addition, the Vindolandan material provides testimony of a few other instances of 'religious consumption:' tablet **180** (quoted above in its entirety, p. 27) had an entry labelled 'likewise [wheat] to Amabilis at the shrine, *modii* 3;'[25] tablet **265** reveals how Cerialis encouraged a friend to 'consecrate the day of the Kalends [New Year's Day] by sacrifice;' tablet **301** (to be treated below, p. 40) is a letter between household slaves concerning commodities to be purchased for an upcoming religious holiday; and, finally, tablet **313** is a fragment which seems to concern a meeting between a priest and a prefect about arrangements for a festival—a coordination of activities which must also have been relevant for Cerialis' 'expenses *ad sacrum*.'

---

[15] The rank of prefect of an auxiliary cohort was reserved for Roman citizens of equestrian status, that is, of men whose fortune amounted to at least 400,000 *sestertii*, and who belonged to the social tier just below the senatorial order; see, for instance, Frere, *Britannia*, pp. 186, 208.
[16] *Tab.Vindol.* II.291, III.622, 629.
[17] *Tab.Vindol.* II.292 and 257.
[18] *Tab.Vindol.* II.250.
[19] *Tab.Vindol.* II.225 and 248, respectively.
[20] Bowman, *Life and Letters*, p. 40; and R. Birley, *A Roman Frontier Fort*, p. 71; both consider this issue, although only very briefly.
[21] Seeing that the first three lines of fragment (c) probably relate to expenses for a festival on 18th June, it is possible that the cohort celebrated the little known '*Annae sacrum*;' cf. A. Pauly and G. Wissowa (eds), *Paulys Realencyclopädie der classischen Altertumswissenschaft*, rev. edn, vol. I.2 (Stuttgart, 1958), s.v. 'Anna,' p. 2224, l. 64.
[22] *Tab.Vindol.* II.190, ll. 29–30: *axungiae (sextarios) x mut[(uo)] domino ad stipes*.
[23] *Tab.Vindol.* II.190, l. 32: *vini m(odium) i ad sacrum d<i>vae*.
[24] Cf. H. H. Scullard, *Festivals and Ceremonies of the Roman Republic* (London, 1981), p. 155. Besides, there is also an altar stone dedicated to *Fortuna*, albeit probably of a later date: *RIB* I, 1,684.
[25] *Tab.Vindol.* II.180, l. 10: *item Amabili ad fanum m(odii) iii*.

However, this rather fragmented picture of religious life and expenditure at Vindolanda can be supplemented with the *Feriale Duranum* of *Dura-Europus*, dating from AD 225–35.[26] This unique document, of which little more than half has survived in a well-preserved state, constitutes a later edition of the Augustan standard list of festivals prescribed for all the armies of the *Imperium Romanum*. Thus, the *Feriale* applied to all military units —that is to say, to legionaries and auxiliaries alike—and must have played a role in a process of Romanisation which exposed foreign soldiers like the Tungrians and Batavians to the gods and principal holidays of Rome, as well as to the cult of the emperors.[27] And there were, in fact, quite a number of prescribed celebrations: if the ordained sacrifices were to be carried out according to the letter, a cohort like that at *Dura-Europus* or at *Vindolanda* would have had to expend forty-two heads of cattle (variously specified as either oxen, cows or bulls) annually on matters of state religion alone![28]

Significantly, the festivals on 18th June and 24th June, which Cerialis made donations for, are not to be found in the *Feriale*. Furthermore, celebrations in honour of Germanic deities 'imported' by the Batavians (and the Tungrians) from their homeland on the Rhine are also likely to have been performed.[29] The implication is, therefore, that the 9th cohort of Batavians celebrated all the events prescribed in the official, military *Feriale*, but that they also continued to pay homage to both other Roman gods as well as their own native gods (which is really not surprising, the polytheistic and including nature of Roman religion considered), thus ensuring an annual 'religious consumption' of forty-two bovines in addition to whatever means and resources which may have been expended on celebrations for other Roman, local and ethnic deities.

In conclusion, the reciprocal expenses prompted by religion should not be underestimated: state religion, 'public' religion and the private religion of the inhabitants of the fort (be they soldiers, civilians or slaves) merged to create a steady demand for objects of religious consumption. Thus, although the state-ordained sacrifices of the *Feriale* may have been paid for out of the cohort's coffers, the evidence certainly also attests to private expenditure of means for religious purposes— transforming religious activities into becoming economic activities, as well.

Tab.Vindol. II.**255**, in translation:

> Clodius Super to his Cerialis, greetings. I was pleased that our friend Valentinus on his return from Gaul has duly approved the clothing. Through him I greet you and ask that you send me the things which I need for the use of my boys, that is, six *sagaciae*, n *saga*, seven *palliola*, tunics; in fact, you know that I am smart in getting hold of this since I am the commissariat officer and am now on the point of acquiring transport. (2nd hand) May you fare well, my dearest and most longed for lord and brother.
> (Back, 1st hand) To Flavius Cerialis, prefect, from Clodius Super, centurion.[30]

A centurion has written to Cerialis, whom we encountered in the case study above, through an intermediary who was a friend of both, requesting that he be sent an amount of specified clothing for his personal slaves.[31] This messenger and common friend, Valentinus, had approved 'the clothing on his return from Gaul,' but whether this means that he approved of a consignment of clothes in Gaul, which were then to be sent to Vindolanda, or he had approved of a consignment of clothes for the fort *in* Britain *after* his return from Gaul (where he may have been on various kinds of errands), is impossible to tell.[32]

What we do know, though, is that Clodius Super was leaving soon, having been appointed to a new position, and that he was therefore in need of these specific items of clothing for his slaves before going on his travels.[33] Furthermore, in asking for them he made no mention of any kind of remuneration, nor did he write that the granting of this favour would put him under a social obligation to Cerialis. On the other hand, the letter does contain plenty of 'endearment phrases,' not least the closing greeting's 'may you fare well, my dearest and most longed for lord and brother,'[34] which is rather surprising, considering that this was a centurion addressing an equestrian officer.

However, it all makes sense if this was an embedded transaction based on personal relations and not merely on the official relationship between a centurion and his prefect: a small consignment of specified textiles was requested in a private capacity, for these clothes were not

---

[26] *P.Dura-Europus* 54.
[27] Cf. discussion in Welles *et al.*, *The Excavations at Dura-Europus*, pp. 193–97.
[28] Marichal, *Ostraca*, p. 105.
[29] Quite a number of altar stones dedicated to Germanic deities have been found at Vindolanda: *RIB* I, 1,683, 1,692, 1,697–99, 1,722a, 1,722d–f.
[30] *Tab.Vindol.* II, p. 224; and with extensive amendments from the Appendix of *Tab.Vindol.* III, p. 157. *Tab.Luguval.* 24 may contain an answer to a similar request.
[31] Although Bowman and Thomas have chosen to translate '*pueri*' as 'boys' instead of 'slaves,' the latter is indeed the standard Classical meaning of the word (which reading they also prefer themselves, as revealed in the notes to ll. 6–8, *Tab.Vindol.* II, p. 226).
[32] A. R. Birley, *Garrison Life*, p. 101, considers the former to be the correct reading, but in my opinion both are possible—*Tab.Vindol.* II.255, ll. i.3–5: [*V*]*alentinum n(ostrum) a Gallia reversum commode vestem adprobasse gratulatus sum*.
[33] The Vindolanda Tablets contain an impressive amount of references to textiles, as is attested in the Appendix, which make up a large part of the evidence for a thorough article on this topic: J. P. Wild, 'The Textile Industries of Roman Britain' in *Britannia*, Vol. 33 (2002), 1–42. On the scraps of textiles uncovered at Vindolanda specifically, see also *VRR* III, pp. 85–86.
[34] *Tab.Vindol.* II.255, ll. ii.14–17 with amendment from *Tab.Vindol.* III, p. 157: *valeas domine frater carissime et desideratissime*.

for soldiers but for Clodius' household staff. Furthermore, Clodius offered to pay or arrange for neither goods nor transport, which left the entire expense of the transaction up to Cerialis, which could be justified only by a bond of friendship or a patron-client relationship of near equality (judging from the tone of the letter).[35] Consequently, this appears to be positive evidence of socially embedded, economic activity.

In fact, several other tablets provide testimony of minor transactions embedded in the relationship between giver and recipient: tablet **196** is a list of garments from Cerialis' *praetorium* with two entries being put down as obtained through named acquaintances, and in tablet **233** Cerialis pleads with a friend to send him hunting-nets; tablets **218** and **667** reveal correspondents helping each other to obtain commodities which either were in need of; and finally, tablet **346** constitutes the covering letter from a package of garments sent to a friend, while **641**, **643** and **667** concern the process of obtaining goods by exploiting personal networks—the common denominator of all the cases cited being that no money seems to have changed hands, everything being settled within the contexts of specific personal relationships.[36]

Tab. Vindol. III.**581**, in translation:

(a) <u>Consumed</u> (?) [my emphasis]
11th (?) April
... the decurion(s)
of the 1st ... beer (?) ...
16th May, (by?) ...
the brewer ...
18th May, by (?) ...
chickens ...
In the 5th consulship of Trajan
26th April ...
by Crescens ...
vacat
on the same day, by ...
a goose ...
(b) 5th June, (by?) ...
Suetius (?) ...
10th June, (by?) ...
the brewer ...
11th June, (by?) ...
Vatto ...
In the consulship of Sex. Attius Suburbanus
1st January, by ...
veteran, chickens ...
on the same day, by Sautenus (?) ...
by Chnisso ...
2nd January ...
chickens ...
(c) 1st March, by Ma...
on the same day, by Candidus (?)
30th March, by Mar...
31st March, by Exsomnius (?) ...
line deleted
23rd April, by V...

in charge of the draft-animals of Brocchus (?)
total, geese ...
likewise, geese ...
nurseling chicks (?) ...
likewise, nurselings (?) ...
chickens ...
30th April
likewise, chickens ...
through Comm ... (?)
total, chickens ...
(d) [date ?]
...
<u>disbursed</u> ... [my emphasis]
18th May ...
... a chicken
on the same day, for ...'s dinner (?) ...
chicken (?) consumed, 1 (?)
25th May ...
..., a chicken ...
13th June ...
of (?) the legate ...
14th June
at Coria, on the instructions of ...
line deleted
on the same day in ...
there have died ...
(e.back) 10th June ...
discharge of Flavinus (?) ...
30th August ...
for Niger and Brocchus ...
25th December
for Brocchus' dinner (?)
1st January, through (?) ...
...
17th January ...
for Brocchus ...
21st February ...
from the pen ...
1st March, for the lord(s) (?) ...
of the Matronalia (?) ...
(d.back) 15th March ...
for Niger and Lae ...
21st March ...
...
4th April ...
for Brocchus ...
29th April, ...
for September ...
4th May ...
with Sautenus ...
total disbursed ...
remainder ...
and geese, number ...
from these (?) ...
(c.back)
9th May ...
for (?) Onesimus with the standards (?) ...
on the same day, for Sautenus ...
in the pen ...
29th May, as lunch for ...

---

[35] Interestingly, *Tab.Vindol.* III.629 could have been written by the same Clodius Super who makes humble excuses for not having attended the birthday party of Cerialis' wife, Lepidina.
[36] Cf. also *O.Claud.* I.177.

>   and Flavinus, consumed (?) ...
>   on the same day, ...
>   with Sautenus ...
>   1st May, for the *singulares* (?)
>   on the visit of the governor ...
>   consumed (?) at lunch ...
>   likewise outside for Myr ... (?)
>   6th June ...
>   chickens, number 4 (?)
> (b.back) 16th July ...
>   through Surenus the *centurion* (?) ...
>   ..., number 12
>   on the same day ...
>   for ...nus (?) chickens ...
>   in the hands of Sautenus ...
>   ..., chickens ...
>   total, chickens, number 20+
>   from these, Tanagrian (?) ...
>   remainder, sterile (?) ...
>   total (?), chickens, number 7+

This tablet constitutes yet another domestic account from Flavius Cerialis' household and should therefore be considered as a sort of running account and tally of the *praetorium*'s poultry.[37] Bowman and Thomas suggest that it was 'compiled retrospectively by a domestic manager' which could explain the account's inconsistent nature and the sizeable gaps in dated entries.[38] Furthermore, they interpret it as consisting of two different parts: tablets (a)–(c) which concern poultry consumed by various persons and maybe paid for (due to the loss of the right hand margins it is impossible to tell whether there were cash sums related to the entries); and tablets (d)–(e.back)–(d.back)–(c.back)–(b.back) which account for poultry disbursed for various reasons. Taken together, the two sections span a considerable period of time, ranging from April, AD 102 to July, AD 104.[39]

Once again, it is the specific context of the account which is of interest: how did the prefect utilise this personal asset, the keeping of poultry, in relation to his role as both commanding officer and private equestrian? The first section is difficult to interpret as we lack any kind of certainty about the nature of the transactions listed—the poultry entered here could have been sold for cash to members of the garrison, but it could also have been handed over as part of payments, salaries or something similar. However, the author of the account had a need to separate the two sections under different headings, so it is not unreasonable to assume that the first section does, indeed, relate to poultry exchanged for cash or services provided.

The second and longer section, then, would be concerned with disbursements or private/semi-official consumption. The individual entries seem to support this view as recipients are now in the dative (whereas section one had '*ab N*'), and details like 'discharge of Flavinus,' 'for Brocchus' dinner' and 'on the visit of the governor' crop up throughout the account.[40] Apparently, section two reveals some of the prefect's social obligations and activities, as we here have indirect evidence of the *praetorium* having hosted discharge festivities, official parties for high-ranking visitors and probably what amounted to friendly dinner parties between Flavius Cerialis and some of his fellow officers. Similar 'embedded consumption' is attested in a tablet where the writer of a letter proudly proclaims that a friend had sent him fifty oysters,[41] and by messages concerned with the details of formal dinners or parties.[42] In addition, a short letter informs us that the soldiers at *Vindonissa* also knew how to have a good time: 'Thus, you may know when I stage the party, various games and neat revelry. Tomorrow, by the mighty guardian spirits of the game, I will shake the dice cup like the sword!'[43]

Interestingly, a small archive of *ostraca* from *Mons Claudianus* all concern the activities of a soldier, Dioscorus,[44] stationed somewhere else than the main garrison, in sending three select friends vegetables from a fertile garden plot he had the opportunity of tending.[45] In the middle of a barren desert, these vegetables must have been prized as supplements to the regular army provisions—which is, indeed, emphasised by Dioscorus' habit of demanding instant letters of acceptance from the recipients—but nowhere does he mention any prices or debts (although he himself enquires about the cost of vinegar and pays for supplies of fish).[46] Thus, this is likely to be more evidence of socially embedded disbursements of food: Dioscorus took advantage of a personal asset, his well-tended garden, to ingratiate himself with his peers.[47]

In conclusion, tablet **581** may provide something as interesting as evidence for market exchange and reciprocity working alongside one another in a casual

---

[37] Similar evidence for the keeping of poultry is provided by *Tab.Vindol.* III.582. On the archaeological remains of poultry at Vindolanda, see *VRR* III, p. 113; and Birley and Blake, *The Excavations of 2005–2006*, p. 178. Moreover, a study of Roman military life in Wales suggests that consumption of geese and chickens may have been the prerogative of officers; see J. L. Davies, 'A Welsh Perspective,' p. 183.
[38] *Tab.Vindol.* III, p. 25.
[39] *Tab.Vindol.* III, pp. 24–25; the two section headings are supposed to be 'accepta ab N,' 'absumpti [sc. pulli]' or 'absumpta ab N' from the surviving, fragmentary 'a..['; and 'expensa' from the better preserved 'expensa[.'
[40] Respectively: *missio Flavi*[(l. 61); *cenanti Brocch*[*o* (l. 64); and *adventu consu*[*laris* (l. 96).
[41] *Tab.Vindol.* II.299.
[42] *Tab.Vindol.* III.617, 666.
[43] *Tab.Vindon.* 45.
[44] Cf. the discussion of the evidence for his military status, Bingen et al., *Mons Claudianus*, p. 44.
[45] *O.Claud.* II.224–42.
[46] *O.Claud.* II.225–27.
[47] Moreover, *O.Claud.* II.370 indicates that this practice was widespread and that members of the garrison could be quite ardent in their pursuit of longed-for vegetables.

manner: on the one hand, the prefect disbursed poultry when and where fitting for his station and in response to the various social obligations placed upon him; and on the other hand, one of his domestic managers exchanged poultry with various individuals who were not entitled to poultry as a 'gift,' but who paid in cash, kind or services instead. Common to these two economic practices is the meticulous manner in which something as relatively inexpensive as poultry was accounted for—chickens for dinner on special occasions may have been embedded transactions, but they were certainly also perceived of as economic assets and therefore recorded.

Conclusions drawn from miscellaneous tablets
This chapter has almost become a case study not only of reciprocity but also of the prefect of the 9th Cohort of Batavians, Flavius Cerialis. By combining different tablets, it has been possible to sketch the way in which spheres of social and economic activity mingled for this man who was both Roman, Batavian, soldier, husband and father.[48]

Two other tablets complete the picture: one in which he wrote from somewhere to his household instructing that 'all of you take good care to see that if any friends come they are suitably entertained,'[49] which tells us that his home was an asset to be used in the service of friends and that hospitality itself can be considered an embedded economic activity. Furthermore, tablet **596** tells us something about this home, the *praetorium*, for it comprises a sort of asset register of what must have been the prefect's belongings and is probably related to Period III, that is, to the time of Cerialis. The commodities listed seem like a rather random assortment, ranging from headbands over bags and bowls to very expensive purple cloth, but the significance of this list lies in the fact that for every item a quantity and a cash value is given: for instance, we find 'bowls, number 4, 3⅞ *denarii* and 1 *as* each, total 15¾ *denarii*.'[50]

This asset register does not seem to have been compiled with a mind to selling the items, but simply appears to be a sort of inventory and an exact summing up of values—nearly every entry deals in multiplications of *denarii*, fractions of *denarii* and *asses*. This use of money would be similar to Polanyi's 'standard use,' that is to say an equating of various commodities to cash sums, not in the sense of exchange value, but in the sense of the aggregate amount of wealth: Cerialis' possessions were considered economic assets that together constituted his estate and personal fortune and which related directly to his own standing as a rich aristocrat, patron and equestrian. Whether the list was written in connection with the purchase of the items or afterwards does not really affect the argument: the important thing is that it was produced in the first place and kept afterwards until the moving out of the cohort and the discarding of archives—that is, the fact of its discovery at Vindolanda would seem to rule out the possibility that the list was compiled prior to departure as a sort of 'baggage receipt.'

Moreover, there are other tablets attesting to the formal and rather ambiguous nature of embedded transactions. Like that of two slave correspondents making arrangements for the upcoming Saturnalia-festival,[51] where the one instructed the other that 'regarding the ... for the *Saturnalia*, I ask you, brother, to see to them at a price of four or six *asses* and radishes to the value of not less than ½ *denarius*.'[52] There is no hint of donation in the name of the divine or personal sacrifice for the benefit of the sacred: all there is, is the question of obtaining the necessary commodities at the right price—although the mention of 'not less than ½ *denarius*' seems to imply that there was a social obligation to spend at least that amount —a mixture, in short, of reciprocity and market exchange.

A mixture, however, which we can also trace in other tablets where people are making use of their social networks to purchase commodities unavailable in their own environs: **310** concerns the process of obtaining a shears in exchange for cash and having it sent to the payer through friends; **312** provides a fragmented glimpse of a number of dealings and transactions within a social network; and **648** may be evidence of civilian business associates drawing upon one another for various purposes and being under some kind of obligation to each other. Furthermore, *Mons Claudianus* yet again provides an interesting parallel: a small kinship group of related soldiers and a woman (who was either a sister or a wife) exchange goods, money and supplies between themselves, acquaintances and business contacts.[53] Accordingly, although we cannot know to what degree social ties overruled the market—by hampering the exigencies of the price-making mechanism—or substituted entirely for market relationships, it does seem highly plausible that many of these transactions were to some extent embedded.

Indeed, this certainly seems to have been the case with what we might term 'reciprocal loans:' money or foodstuffs loaned at no interest to individuals who repaid in kind over time.[54] Since neither mention of normal nor reduced interests are mentioned, we can presume that these loans were provided as services 'free of charge' which would, however, put the recipient in a debt of gratitude vis-à-vis the lender—embedded loans, in other words. Finally, a surviving fragmentary reference to a

---

[48] The evidence for children in the *praetorium* is, however, circumstantial and mainly based on the finds of 'well-made young children's shoes and boots;' R. Birley, *A Roman Frontier Fort*, pp. 75, 87.
[49] *Tab.Vindol.* III.616, ll. A.2–4: *omnes diligenter curate ut si qui am[i]ci venerint bene re[c]ipiantur.*
[50] *Tab.Vindol.* III, p. 55; the original is *Tab.Vindol.* III.596, l. 16: *trullas n(umero) iiii • s(ingularem) • (denarios) iii s(emissem) (quadrantem) (octantem) (assem) i f(iunt) (denarii) xv s(emis) (quadrans).*
[51] *OCD*, s.v. *Saturnus, Saturnalia*: the festival of Saturn, celebrated on 17th December. It was the merriest of all the festivals with plenty of eating, drinking and games, and with normal conduct being inverted, so that slaves could pose as masters.
[52] *Tab.Vindol.* II.301, ll. i.3–6: *souxtum(?) saturnalicum (asses) iiii aut sexs rogo frater explices et radices ne minus (denarii) s(emissem).*
[53] *O.Claud.* I.137–40.
[54] *Tab.Vindol.* II.180 (ll. 5–6), 193, III.586.

debtor who had defaulted on his obligations may reveal how social networks could also be employed to have either friends or superiors bring the debtor back in line.[55]

Conclusion

The evidence of embedded economic activity presented in this chapter has been of a more ambiguous nature than that treated in the two previous chapters. However, given that adequate written testimony of socially determined transactions must necessarily be rather hard to come by, it is perhaps prudent to consider even more thoroughly the implications of the sources treated in the above.

Firstly, evidence of a number of transactions based on the mutual relationship between supplier and recipient has been provided, and in so far as the semi-official nature of our written evidence allows, it has been attested that a great number of social practices with inherent economic significances were taking place at Vindolanda on a daily basis and ranging from the acts of officers to household slaves.

Second, it has been shown that activities which have to be considered as acts of reciprocity were recorded in great detail: the nature of each transaction (whether for religious purposes or somebody's dinner), the quantity expended, often the cash sum equivalent and on what date the transaction took place. Again and again we have seen seemingly trivial and insignificant matters meticulously recorded and accounted for—something which any new description of the Roman economy must therefore take into consideration. The fact that the nature of the evidence is biased towards exactly this kind of conclusion cannot take away from its significance, but only leaves us aware that other aspects of reciprocity may be unattested by the Vindolanda Tablets.

Third, we witness, as we would expect bearing in mind the conclusions from the two previous chapters, that the operation of reciprocity as a way of ordering the exchange of material means within society overlaps with the institution of the market, and, by implication as all the soldiers were paid through the raising of taxes, with the system of redistribution. In particular, the different accounts we have investigated seem to differentiate easily and consistently between economic activities to do with either one or the other of these three modes of economic behaviour. Not because of an awareness of any theory of economics as such, but simply based on the ability to distinguish between the purposes of different transactions: for instance, whether something was for religious use (donations), personal use (asset registration), household use (consumption) or to be sold for cash or disbursed for official purposes.

To sum up, it seems difficult to argue that the Romans had no notion of 'economics' in the sense of the managing of means and measures: the Vindolanda Tablets certainly attest to an economic rationality, albeit one based on a different and broader perception of economic activity than that which is entailed in the modern science of economics. For Flavius Cerialis, every expenditure of either a personal, social, religious or official nature was of economic consequence for the managing of his estate —and he and his domestic managers were acutely aware of it.

In conclusion, the usefulness of a substantivist approach to the ancient economy is borne out by the evidence of these tablets, but they also reveal that the means exchanged through reciprocity were relatively limited compared to the amount of supplies that flowed through redistribution and the institution of the market. However, these particular acts of exchange and consumption were of much greater significance than ordinary transactions, as they served to strengthen the social cohesion of the military community and reinforce certain cultural values. Furthermore, most of the material requirements for these embedded economic activities had to be satisfied in the first instance by goods obtained through either the political economy or the market, and this will have affected the choice of wares available for redistribution and choice of commodities supplied by traders—as will be shown in more detail in the next chapter.

---

[55] *Tab.Vindol.* III.715.

Chapter 6
The Making of a Model:
Layers and Levels of Economic Activity

Layers of economic activity

As it has been argued in the preceding chapters that the Vindolanda Tablets attest to three different kinds of economic activity—that is to say, that the economy as a whole can be conceptualised as consisting of three different layers[1]—the challenge now becomes one of ascertaining the ways in which these layers interact, perform and constitute the 'Vindolandan economy' as a whole. In chapter three, which was concerned with evidence for transactions motivated by economic incentives and conducted through the institution of the market, it was argued that civilian traders and entrepreneurs thrived by supplying various goods to the military community. Numerous exchanges were facilitated by the existence of an extensive cash economy, and transactions between traders on the one hand and every kind of military personnel on the other were recorded as part of the process of exchange. The variety of goods exchanged extended, furthermore, beyond any category of 'supplementary luxury,' as both exotic and mundane wares were sold by the same suppliers.[2]

In considering the people who made use of the market, that is the organisation or economic body that had attuned its activities to gain from this specific kind of exchange,[3] it is useful to differentiate between two different kinds of economic agent (though these roles were sometimes filled by the same person): the trader and the entrepreneur. 'Traders' were those suppliers of wares who made dealings with individuals, mostly in their private capacity, and were sellers of various goods in relatively small quantities to the residents of the fort.[4] This group of economic agents would be dependent on that part of the soldiers' salaries which was actually paid out to them in cash,[5] and which could be converted into extraordinary consumption on a commodities market supplied by these traders.

'Entrepreneurs', on the other hand, were those who supplied whatever products were demanded by the official army supply apparatus in bulk and in expectation of a profit.[6] This group of economic agents could be involved in several different activities at the same time, and did not only act as middlemen, but also processed goods before selling them on. In their involvement with military personnel, both traders and entrepreneurs might also themselves be buyers of goods that the army had in abundant supply—but no matter whether they were sellers or buyers in their dealings with the state, the important thing is that their transactions were conducted via the institution of the market.[7] Nor should it be forgotten that whatever goods these people supplied, they would have had to obtain themselves from a local, inter-regional or even inter-provincial context and, once again, by use of the free market as opposed to the command economy.[8]

In chapter four, evidence for the supply of wares to Vindolanda based on the activities of a political institution, the imperial government, whose responsibility it was to keep the Roman armies in the field was assessed, and the conclusions arrived at were that state redistribution based on the expenditure of taxes could be conducted through either army or civilian channels, which implies the existence of two different organisations and different ways of obtaining supplies.[9] Furthermore, we saw that the nature of these transactions was highly formal, both where it concerned a well-organised army apparatus and where the process of redistribution was carried out in an *ad hoc* way by use of civilian middlemen. All in all, the command economy of Vindolanda is attested as having been of a highly dynamic and flexible nature: if goods were needed, and not in the supply of the army itself, they could be obtained through the market where cash was simply expended by the individual officials in charge of the relevant areas, or a specific supply operation was outsourced to a civilian contractor in its entirety.

However, it is also important to keep in mind the economic consequences of this empire-wide redistributive system, for not only did it cause goods to be moved about on a wide scale, from the import of Baetican olive oil and wine from the Rhône valley to the quarrying and carting around of supplies of local stone,[10] but it also supplied the salaries without which skilled

---

[1] In order to maintain a clear distinction between the nature and scale of economic activity, the former will presently be analysed in terms of 'layers,' whereas the latter, in the next section, will be described in terms of 'levels.'
[2] Cf. for instance *Tab.Vindol.* II.184 in which pepper and tallow are sold by the same supplier.
[3] Cf. North, *Institutions*, p. 4–5.
[4] Traders are attested in *Tab.Vindol.* II.181, 182, 184, 186, 192, IV.i.861.
[5] As much as two thirds of it might have been deducted for mandatory disbursements of food and equipment, see Rodriguez, 'Baetica and Germania,' p. 296; and Whittaker, 'Supplying the Army,' p. 229.
[6] Entrepreneurs are attested in *Tab.Vindol.* II.343, 344 (in conjunction with 180) and III.645.
[7] For people who both sold and bought, see: *Tab.Vindol.* II.182, 186 and 343; in the latter, the two partners may have purchased a large consignment of hides from the army tanneries at Catterick, but although they may also only have been acting as contractors transporting the hides, this is rendered somewhat unlikely by the fact that the military partner was to supply the wagon needed.
[8] Take, for instance, *Tab.Vindol.* II.184, where the range of goods sold extends from tallow to pepper; and *Tab.Vindol.* II.302, in which a slave is sent to purchase among other things eggs and olives.
[9] Contrast *Tab.Vindol.* II.180 with *Tab.Luguval.* 1A; *Tab.Vindol.* III.607 with IV.i.862; and *Tab.Vindol.* IV.i.861 with *Tab.Luguval.* 16.
[10] For finds of these commodities, see R. Birley, *Vindolanda: Extraordinary Records*, pp. 36, 40; and for the reference to quarrying and transport, *Tab.Vindol.* II.316.

Roman soldiers would not have engaged upon a host of tasks which developed the infrastructure of Roman Britain to a very high level,[11] and without which the demand of the soldiers for various goods not supplied by the state could not have created a market for private expenditure and consumption.[12]

The manner in which the taxes, upon which this redistributive system was based, were raised is also a matter of interest, for if the taxes levied in Britain were raised in cash, and not in kind as 'grain-tax,' then they would have forced farmers throughout the province to integrate themselves into local cash-based market economies, and the army would then have had to obtain the grain it needed from other sources: either the free market or by purchase at fixed prices—a practice which would amount, in reality, to an extra grain-tax with some remuneration involved.[13]

Lastly, the fifth chapter dealt with exchanges based on various social practices, in particular those of one of the prefects of Vindolanda.[14] It was argued that there is, indeed, positive evidence for the existence of an embedded economy within the military community, and that transactions conducted for social purposes were recorded in the same way as any other economic transactions, whether private or official, market-based or redistributive, which would seem to grant this specific type of economic activity a kind of formal rationality of its own. It is also evident, though, that whatever means were expended for social purposes had been obtained either through the official army supply apparatus or through the market, which made this kind of economic activity dependent upon the existence, in subservient roles, of its counterparts.[15]

However, neither should it be forgotten that in considering that layer of the economy in which factors of reciprocity governed the exchange of goods, it is more true than ever that economic activities were also social practices and *vice versa*; meaning that although goods were obtained through other economic mechanisms, they were obtained, used and expended for social reasons. Based on this argument, reciprocity should not be seen as an 'inferior' mediator of exchange compared to redistribution and the market, but rather the other way around: factors embedded within Roman society as social practices determined which goods were to be the objects of redistribution, no matter the distance between recipients and Mediterranean producers, and traders regarded 'conspicuous consumption' as just another source of opportunity—as just another market from which they could make a profit.[16]

For these reasons, any model of the economy of Vindolanda must first and foremost try to capture this complex nature of the evidence: the fact that there was no such thing as one Vindolandan economy—rather on the contrary, three different economic mechanisms were being employed by the same people for different purposes. Therefore, we can speak only of one aggregate economy in the sense that it refers to the way in which market exchange, redistribution and reciprocity intersected. If, however, we were to analyse this system as it is revealed in the Vindolanda Tablets, the result would be as follows:

1) An empire-wide redistributive system supplied Vindolanda with cash and maybe taxes in kind (primarily grain, maybe cattle).[17] The tablets provide surprisingly little evidence of how this state supply-mechanism actually worked, but the fort must have received cash for the soldier's salaries, and the remains of Baetican olive oil amphorae, La Graufesenque pottery and wine barrels from the Rhône valley[18] imply integration into a state-subsidised supply network which supplied commodities that could not be obtained by the army itself in the frontier provinces, as argued by numerous authors over the years.[19]

---

[11] Firstly, the cash needed for these salaries was allocated to each military unit by the provincial governor, see Monfort, 'The Roman Military Supply,' pp. 74–75; second, *Tab.Vindol.* II.242 probably concerns the payment of salaries; and thirdly, see *Tab.Vindol.* II.155, 156 for work on infrastructure—*Tab.Vindol.* II.258 may even concern the construction of a bridge.

[12] A prime example of the private consumerism of soldiers is *Tab.Vindol.* II.184, which also informs us that these fresh converts to Roman culture must have prized trips to the bathhouse: several buy towels.

[13] The activities of the three entrepreneurs attested in chapter three (*Tab.Vindol.* III.343, 344, III.645) can be interpreted as purchasing grain from farmers who were trying to raise money for paying taxes; *Tab.Vindol.* III.649 is often quoted in favour of taxes in kind or requisition of grain, but due to its fragmented state it is highly ambiguous and can really only be used as firm evidence for the supply of grain in the frontier zone and natives supplying transport service—however, Tacitus mentions *frumenti et tributorum exactio* (*Agricola* 19.4), and he makes the native chieftain Calgacus say that *bona fortunaeque in tributum, ager atque annus in frumentum* (...) *conteruntur* (*Agricola* 31.1), although in an earlier paragraph Tacitus only speaks of *dilectum ac tributa et iniuncta imperii munera* (*Agricola* 13.1).

[14] *Tab.Vindol.* II.190, 255, III.581.

[15] The picture might have looked very different had the tablets concerned themselves with primary producers; as it is, the only possible exemptions from this dependency on other means of exchange are the poultry-accounts, *Tab.Vindol.* II.581–82, since residents (probably slaves) must have raised and kept the poultry.

[16] Bowman argues that the Germanic officers were facsimile of the Roman élite, but that we do not know how the rank and file perceived of Roman culture; Bowman, *Life and Letters*, p. 79. However, it can be argued that nearly all soldiers in the tablets have adopted Roman first names and many purchase goods which reflect *Romanitas*; see Appendix.

[17] For grain-taxes, see P. Erdkamp, 'The Corn Supply of the Roman Armies During the Principate (27 BC–235 AD),' in P. Erdkamp (ed.), *The Roman Army and the Economy* (Amsterdam, 2002), pp. 54, 59; and Whittaker, 'Supplying the Army,' p. 228; for cattle, Richmond, *Roman Britain*, pp. 132–33; and Frere, *Britannia*, p. 216.

[18] For Baetican olive oil and wine from the Rhône valley, see above, n. 10, p. 42; for Graufesenque pottery, cf. *VRR* I, pp. 19–22: the deposit dates from c. AD 90 and the consignment was apparently dumped unused due to having sustained minor damage *en route*.

[19] Most recently in this specific context by Monfort, 'The Roman Military Supply,' pp. 80, 82; Whittaker, 'Supplying the army,' p. 211–12; and P. P. A. Funari, 'The Consumption of Olive Oil in Roman Britain and the Role of the Army,' in P. Erdkamp (ed.), *The Roman Army and the Economy* (Amsterdam, 2002), p. 244. Also of some interest are D. Williams and C. Carreras, 'North African Amphorae in Roman Britain: A Re-Appraisal,' in *Britannia*, Vol. 26 (1995), pp. 236–37; and D. P. S. Peacock and D. F. Williams, *Amphorae and the Roman Economy* (London and New York, 1986), pp. 57–63.

2) A market for bulk produce not supplied by the official army supply system grew up around Vindolanda in the decades following the establishment of the fort, and we witness the activities of entrepreneurs, dealing mainly in grain, who not only did business with the army, but also supplied it under terms of contract.[20]

3) The garrison of the fort was employed in tasks in the local area, and while one part of the salaries expended on the soldiers thereby contributed to the overall political economy in the form of productive labour, the other part contributed in an indirect way by being payment for the policing duties that stabilised the frontier zone[21] and made development and prosperity possible in the north of the province.[22]

4) The way individual soldiers chose to spend whatever part of their salary which was paid out to them in cash created an 'embedded economy' where means were expended as conspicuous consumption fitting to the status of the individual and economic behaviour interacted with social and religious practices in general. However, this layer of economic activity based on reciprocity was only made possible by the wages and wares supplied by the redistributive system and by the market for specific commodities that grew up as traders responded to the demand exerted by the aggregate purchasing power of the garrison.[23]

Through the lens provided by the Vindolanda Tablets we can dimly perceive an economic system the nature of which was split between three different ways of ordering the exchange of means within society: a political economy provided the basis for the existence of the military community and intersected with a market economy which provided it with goods that could be obtained more cost-efficiently from local sources than by subsiding long-distance imports;[24] soldiers, deriving their wages from this political economy, developed the local infrastructure and created the basis for a market catering for those of their needs which were not met by the flow of goods channelled by political redistribution;[25] and finally, the way in which the various members of the garrison acted as consumers was determined by social considerations such as rank, status, religious and communal obligations (all of which were necessarily interrelated) and thereby constituted an embedded economy where social practices were also economic practices.

Levels of economic activity
This study has been focused mainly on identifying different modes of economic behaviour in the Vindolanda Tablets, but in doing so a certain amount of evidence relating to matters of scale in the ancient economy has also been dealt with. In order to appreciate better the relative importance of each of the different ways of institutionalising economic activities at Vindolanda, a brief enquiry into the scale on which these institutions worked will therefore be conducted below.[26]

On the lowest level, the local one, Vindolanda was the focus of much activity. Skilled soldiers carried out a number of tasks in the immediate vicinity of the fort, which implies that the specific command economy of Vindolanda used its own garrison to supply itself as best it could: we have evidence of building activity, quarrying, various kinds of manufacture, animal husbandry and mining.[27] At the same time, there is evidence for a market in perishable foodstuffs such as oysters and shell-fish, fruit, vegetables and meat (both from domesticated animals and from hunting), which implies that these commodities must have been obtainable within a fairly local context.[28] Furthermore, social activities and the expenses they entailed, involving members of the garrison in general, a prefect and local commanders from other military establishments in the surrounding area, are well attested, as are donations for religious ceremonies at

---

[20] Cf. the 'entrepreneurial activity' attested in chapter three and redistributive processes employing civilians in chapter four.

[21] Cf. the evidence provided in chapter four for army manufacture, production and policing operations.

[22] K. Greene, *The Archaeology of the Roman Economy* (London, 1986), p. 126: the density of farmsteads south of the later Hadrian's Wall is three times higher than to the north of it; see B. Jones and D. Mattingly, *An Atlas of Roman Britain* (Oxford, 1993), maps 7:3 and 7:22, for distributions of evidence for Celtic field systems and native settlements in the northern frontier region, respectively. Moreover, Tacitus tells us that: 'In order that scattered, primitive and warlike people would become accustomed to peace and quiet through the joys of life, Agricola encouraged individuals and aided communities, so that they would construct temples, *fora* and houses' and 'gradually they strayed into tempting vices: the colonnade, the bath and sophisticated revelry' (*Agricola* 21.1–2).

[23] Cf. the arguments in chapter five for the economic significance of certain social activities, and the evidence of traders dealing directly with various individuals in chapter three.

[24] That is, the political economy sought to reduce transaction costs by making use of the institution of the market when and where possible; cf. the discussion of the inherent economising rationale of redistribution and reciprocity in D. North, 'Markets and Other Allocation Systems in History: The Challenge of Karl Polanyi,' in *Journal of European Economic History*, 6 (1977), 709, 715.

[25] The system described so far corresponds well with Bowman's view on the economy of Vindolanda; see Bowman, *Life and Letters*, pp. 70, 72; and compare with his more recent sketch of the Vindolandan economy in A. K. Bowman, 'Outposts of Empire: Vindolanda, Egypt and the Empire of Rome,' in *Journal of Roman Archaeology*, 19 (2006), pp. 82–86.

[26] A good, recent account of research on the nature of distribution-mechanisms in the early Empire is provided by N. Morley, 'The Early Roman Empire: Distribution,' in W. Scheidel, R. Saller and I. Morris (eds), *The Cambridge Economic History of the Greco-Roman World* (Cambridge, 2007), pp. 580–589, 591; although Morley's use of *Tab.Vindol.* II.192, 218 (p. 585, n. 77) to attest to civilian transport contractors in army employ is open to other interpretations: for instance, that *Tab.Vindol.* II.192 concerns *praetorium* consumption and supply by traders, whilst *Tab.Vindol.* II.218 is highly ambiguous but concerns private consumption and the use of messengers and social networks—however, none of them contain references to transport as such. Moreover, the account which follows compares well to that of Bowman, *Life and Letters*, pp. 45–48.

[27] For building activity, *Tab.Vindol.* II.155, 156; for quarrying, *Tab.Vindol.* II.316 and A. R. Birley, *Garrison Life*, pp. 49, 56, 93; for some examples of manufacturers: shoemakers, *Tab.Vindol.* II.155, III.604; carpenters, *Tab.Vindol.* II.309, III.600; a shield-maker, *Tab.Vindol.* II.184; brewers, *Tab.Vindol.* II.182, III.581; for animal husbandry, *Tab.Vindol.* II.180, III.581; and finally, for mining, *Tab.Vindol.* II.155, and R. Birley, *Vindolanda: Extraordinary Records*, pp. 38, 44.

[28] For oysters (which can actually be transported surprisingly far) and shell-fish generally, *Tab.Vindol.* II.299 and *VRR* III, p. 114; for fruit and vegetables, *Tab.Vindol.* II.192, 204, 301, 302, III.591, 592; for meat, *Tab.Vindol.* II.182, 186, 191, III.581, 587, 592; moreover, 'the frequency of meat according to species was beef, mutton, pork, goat, venison, bird, fish, shellfish and molluscs,' see *VRR* III, p. 109.

Vindolanda.²⁹

One level higher, we can tell that entrepreneurs and traders must have acted on an intra-provincial level, as they were able to secure both large quantities of raw materials as well as large varieties of processed or fabricated goods—something which might have been possible to do within a limited radius of Vindolanda, but which their roles as mobile middlemen imply could not be obtained by the stationary members of the garrison.³⁰ Some of the activities of these civilian economic agents were motivated by the private demand of soldiers, others by the official needs of the fort, and so an intermittent demand for supplies permanently or temporarily unobtainable was probably satisfied in this way.³¹ Nor should we forget that the correspondence of Cerialis provides testimony of a far-flung social network which could and did make demands on his personal resources.³²

For the scale of activities at the highest level, that of the imperial economic framework, the Vindolanda Tablets yield very little evidence. However, some accounts do contain entries about wine, olives, olive oil, fish-sauce and pepper, which must necessarily have been imported to Britain from warmer provinces.³³ The question is, though, how these goods reached Vindolanda: were they directed to the frontier by the direct action of the political economy or by hefty subsidies? Or did they find their way to the military market simply by the overwhelming forces of supply and demand which the frontier forces exerted? One tablet tells us that what we must presume to be a *praetorium* slave was sent on an errand to purchase among other things olives and fish-sauce,³⁴ and there are several instances of tablets recording the purchase of wine in private or official functions, but these scattered references can hardly account for the supply of Mediterranean commodities to the whole cohort. The only conclusion inferable from the Vindolanda Tablets would be that some of these wares did actually find their way to the fort as commercial goods.

In summary, it would seem that each of the three exchange mechanisms operated on both a local, provincial and imperial level. Redistribution is the most obvious case with tax-money having been spent on the necessary army supplies at each different level, but also with the payment of salaries, possible channelling of taxes in kind and subsidising of the production and transport of Mediterranean staples. The institution of the market supplemented these redistributive processes in their different logistical and geographical contexts, and in some cases it is even difficult to distinguish between redistributive elements and market exchange in a meaningful way.³⁵ Lastly, the very fact that an embedded economy obtained its necessary means via redistribution and the market had serious implications for the whole economic system: wares chosen by the Roman state for official redistribution were markers of allegiance or ethnic affiliation (the consumption of olive oil and wine being considered an essentially Roman phenomenon) for those who wished to identify with Roman culture and the ideal of *Romanitas*,³⁶ and demand for this category of commodities would also have caused them to be directed through free market channels.³⁷ In this way, conspicuous consumption within a system of economic reciprocity can be said to interact with economic processes on both a local, provincial and imperial level as well.³⁸

As a supplement to this brief discussion of the geographical scale of the economic activities attested in the Vindolanda Tablets, a map is provided below showing places mentioned explicitly in the tablets and areas of special significance (see **Fig. 4**).³⁹

There are many other issues to do with the scale of Roman army supply in particular and the ancient economy in general, however, to which the evidence from Vindolanda does not speak. Hence, it is of vital importance not to mistake lack of evidence for positive evidence of anything and instead to focus on those aspects of economic life in antiquity to which the tablets actually do bear witness.

---

[29] *Tab.Vindol.* II.190, III.581.
[30] Consider the distances implied in the letters of Octavius and Maior, *Tab.Vindol.* II.343, III.645.
[31] It is almost impossible to say anything about the degree of integration between different markets on the basis of the Vindolanda Tablets alone, but an economic system such as the one proposed here would imply that local, regional and provincial markets were neither fully fragmented nor integrated—that is not saying much, but it is all the available evidence can bear.
[32] Particularly *Tab.Vindol.* II.255, where a favour is asked of Flavius Cerialis, but also *Tab.Vindol.* II.233, where he in turn asks another friend to send him hunting-nets.
[33] *Tab.Vindol.* II.184, 185, 190, 202, 203, 208, 302, III.589, 673, 679.
[34] *Tab.Vindol.* II.302.
[35] Compare with the work of P. F. Bang on this topic: Bang, *The Roman Bazaar*, pp. 62, 68–69, 119, 121–22; and also the North-inspired analysis of Elio Lo Cascio, 'The Role of the State in the Roman Economy: Making Use of the New Institutional Economics' in P. F. Bang, M. Ikeguchi and H. G. Ziche (eds), *Ancient Economies: Modern Methodologies. Archaeology, Comparative History, Models and Institutions* (Bari, 2006), pp. 215–34. Moreover, Ward-Perkins has recently argued forcefully for the primacy of the free market over state redistribution, which was, however, also of considerable importance; see Ward-Perkins, *The Fall of Rome*, pp. 102, 132.
[36] For the ideological implications of certain foodstuffs, both in relation to private consumer and official, government-decreed supply, see Monfort, 'The Roman Military Supply,' p. 71–72. See also Pearce, 'Food as Substance and Symbol,' p. 941.
[37] A prime example is *Tab.Vindon.* 47 which reveals that a wine merchant had chosen to settle in the *vicus* of *Vindonissa*.
[38] Although the concept of 'conspicuous consumption' was first introduced in T. Veblen, *The Theory of the Leisure Class* (New York, 1899), it has also been treated more recently in P. Bourdieu, *Distinction: A Social Critique of the Judgement of Taste* (London, 1984), especially pp. 100–1. Compare this argument with that of Morley, 'The Early Roman Empire: Distribution,' p. 574.
[39] As most of the tablets uncovered are either accounts of some sort, drafts, or letters sent to Vindolanda (without sender's address enclosed), very few place names are attested—and the places that some of these refer to (*Bremesio, Briga, Cordonovis*(?) and *Ulucium*) are as yet unknown. For Vardullian cavalrymen, see *Tab.Vindol.* II.181, l. 13.

Fig. 4: Vindolanda: External Links

The economy of Vindolanda: different perspectives
Studies of the Vindolanda Tablets have mostly been focused on Vindolanda in particular, the frontier, 'military life' or 'the Roman army and the economy.' However, as will be argued in the following, it is more surprising that so few have as yet grasped the potential significance of the Vindolanda Tablets for our understanding of Roman economic *behaviour* in general.

In 1994 C. R. Whittaker published a work in which he presented an economic model of the Roman frontiers by comparing various border zones from all over the Empire. His basic assumption was that frontiers eventually settled where they did due to the marginality of the land in the border zone, the costs of extending the borders of the Empire beyond these limits outweighing the gains.[40] The consequence of this, however, was that the garrisons in the frontier zones could not sustain themselves, and therefore had to import more or less every kind of necessity from further afield.[41]

It is the nature of this importing which is of great interest, for according to Whittaker groups of *negotiatores* or *contractores* (traders or contractors) bid for public contracts to supply the army and thereby linked military demand with the supply of various producers in the provinces.[42] These middlemen would enter into contracts with state officials or even with individual military units, and it would then be their responsibility to procure the relevant supplies and transport them to their final destination (exempt from tax and duties), making use of the army's transport infrastructure and giving any extra, private goods of the contractor a free 'piggy-back ride' to a remote military market.[43]

The model then further suggested how any such frontier zone would prosper because of the contribution of the military economy to the local market economy, especially due to the fact that the army would have exploited any opportunities of obtaining supplies locally, from the frontier zone itself. Accordingly, this would have developed neighbouring regions beyond the frontier through the impact of a substantial 'frontier trade,' whereas the un-Romanised nature of the highland region of Northern Britain, behind the frontier, was to be explained by 'intense rural exploitation' by the army.[44]

As a general framework, this model appears plausible and in its basic assumptions about the workings of the Roman economy it has a lot in common with Hopkins' theory of the reciprocal relationship between taxes and trade in the Roman Empire.[45] However, in a more recent article, Whittaker has dealt with the evidence for army supply from Vindolanda specifically and reached some conclusions which fit the model of his *magnum opus* quite well—but other interpretations of the *corpus* of tablets are possible and point to rather different conclusions.

First of all, the article concludes that there is 'a hint' of evidence that 'while private entrepreneurs were prominent, the traditional involvement of the army and military and imperial administration is still *highly visible* [my italics]'[46]—however, this conclusion is based mainly on circumstantial evidence, primarily wider archaeological studies, and only three tablets are quoted in its favour. Moreover, the evidence of possible state involvement in these tablets is highly ambiguous;[47] especially if they are compared to tablets attesting to the multifarious ways in which private traders and entrepreneurs were engaged in the exchange of goods. In short, the involvement of army-, military- and imperial administration may have been crucial in employing civilians to support the garrison, but it is not something which is 'highly visible' in the Vindolanda Tablets.

Secondly, the article concludes that 'in Britain there seems no doubt that most supplies came from long distances,' although it does allow for the fact that some amount of grain supplies were collected locally.[48] However, this statement is based on the argument that most of the transport concerning food and equipment attested in the tablets refers 'only to movement from a nearby depot to the camp'[49]—in support of which the article refers to no tablets; rather, it implies that the mention of *Cataractonium* (Catterick), *Coria* (Corbridge), *Luguvalium* (Carlisle), *Londinium* (London) and Gaul in other contexts is enough to prove the point; and further, the article goes on to discuss several possibilities for obtaining enough grain within a local, northern context, but *de facto* ends up closing the discussion by stating that 'if we accept the general proposition that Roman frontiers always advanced into zones where they could sustain themselves no further, then strictly local production was never likely to be enough to meet the total needs of military consumption.'[50]

Finally, arguing that the lack of archaeological evidence of Roman trade with farmsteads south of the later Hadrian's Wall underlines the underdeveloped nature of the northern frontier, the conclusion on the whole matter

---

[40] Whittaker, *Frontiers*, p. 86–87.
[41] Whittaker, *Frontiers*, p. 101.
[42] Quite interestingly, Erdkamp argues that Whittaker is wrong in his interpretation of his key source on the existence of *negotiatores*; Erdkamp, 'The Corn Supply of the Roman Armies,' p. 55.
[43] Whittaker, *Frontiers*, pp. 108, 112.
[44] Whittaker, *Frontiers*, pp. 113–14, 128.
[45] Hopkins, 'Rome, Taxes, Rents and Trade,' p. 210.
[46] Whittaker, 'Supplying the army,' p. 233.
[47] *Tab.Vindol.* III.645, II.185, 255; cf. my interpretation of these tablets, pp. 19f, 31, and 37, respectively.
[48] Whittaker, 'Supplying the Army,' p. 233.
[49] Whittaker, 'Supplying the Army,' p. 222.
[50] Whittaker, 'Supplying the Army,' p. 226.

is that the evidence for local entrepreneurs can relate only to 'supplementary provisions'[51]—more likely, however, it simply highlights gaps in our present knowledge.

I would hesitate to claim that there is 'no doubt' that most army supplies came from long distances, when the evidence in favour of this argument is circumstantial and not actually based on the Vindolanda Tablets themselves, which, on the contrary, attest to a plentiful market for grain in the North, where the army had so much grain that it was selling off the surplus and civilians could enter the market freely as both buyers and sellers—this does not imply scarcity even in the early years of the frontier.[52]

Moreover, stating that 5,000 *modii* of spelt grain is to be considered supplementary provisions is extremely misleading, as a small calculation will prove: the letter from Octavius is from Period IV when the 1st Cohort of Tungrians had returned to Vindolanda, and tablet **154**, a strength report of this very cohort dating from Period I, informs us that out of a nominal strength of just below 800 men it was apparently quite normal for only 300 of them to be physically present, as the rest were detailed to specific duties in other places.[53] Using the wheat equivalent of 1/7 modius per man per day, Octavius' consignment of spelt wheat would therefore be enough to feed a 300 strong cohort, on grain alone, for 116 days! It is most unlikely that these were mere 'supplementary provisions.' The letter contains, furthermore, no references or allusions which imply that the purchase was of grain from an early 'villa economy of the South,' and hence, does not support the proposition that army supply was long-distance.[54]

The article is rounded off with two other conclusions, namely that an extensive cash economy was functioning within the military community, but that the native Britons to the north and south were excluded from it, and finally, that there 'is reasonably good cause to think' that the trading activities of the Roman army encouraged growth and development beyond the frontier.[55] While I can only agree with the former conclusion, as there is plenty of evidence in the tablets to support it, the latter is based on pottery shards, similar types of material evidence and inference, and no tablets are quoted in its favour.[56]

In consequence, although Whittaker's arguments are ingenious, they run against the grain of the evidence, for even though the evidence of the Vindolanda Tablets permits a range of interpretations, the main thrust of the *corpus* actually points towards different conclusions. In other words, the view on army supply at Vindolanda laid out in the article may be right, as there is nothing in the tablets which rules out this interpretation as such, but they do not offer any real support for this model. On the contrary, an enquiry based on the Vindolanda Tablets alone leads to different results, as accounted for in both the above discussion and the two former parts of this chapter, and hence, they should force us to reconsider the roles of local, entrepreneurial civilians over official state involvement in supply, the importance of local markets for grain over long-distance import, and the peculiar lack of attested interaction between natives and Romans in the frontier zone.[57]

A view more in keeping with that adopted in this chapter —and Whittaker's original frontier model—is advanced in what may well be the most thorough article to date on Spanish olive oil imports to Roman Britain. In this article, P. P. A. Funari argues that the needs of the Roman army were met by a combination of local supplies and long-distance imports, as the Vindolanda Tablets are 'replete with entrepreneurial initiative' while the archaeological remains of wares such as imported Baetican olive oil abound all over the province as well.[58] Based on an extensive analysis of the available archaeological evidence for the import of this particular type of Mediterranean staple, Funari concludes that the military supply system was the result of the free market being intertwined with political redistribution, whereby market trade of Baetican oil became a side-effect of the strategic production and transportation encouraged by the state, as some exporters in Baetica chose to focus on civilian markets rather than enter into contractual agreements with the military.[59]

On the other hand, articles by P. Erdkamp and C. C. Monfort stress the grounding of the supply of staples in the structure of Roman state officialdom, as they argue for the active role of an imperial *praefectus annonae* in Rome whose task it was to supervise the allocation of inter-provincial supplies like grain, olive oil, wine and the like.[60] This central head of the supply system would then coordinate with the governor of each province and the *procuratores Augusti*, and together they would see to it that as many supplies as possible could be obtained

---

[51] Whittaker, 'Supplying the Army,' pp. 229–30; echoed by Erdkamp, 'The Corn Supply of the Roman Armies,' p. 67.
[52] Cf., in particular, *Tab.Vindol.* II.180 (in conjunction with 344), 213, 343, 348, III.645, 649
[53] *Tab.Vindol.* II.154.
[54] On the contrary, Octavius complains that the roads had been too bad for him to go to Catterick, so it is not likely that he had obtained this considerable amount of grain from very far away, and the tablet does not provide grounds for thinking that he might have had access to sea transport; *Tab.Vindol.* II.343.
[55] Whittaker, 'Supplying the Army,' p. 234.
[56] Britons are only mentioned in *Tab.Vindol.* II.164, which could be a report on the military prowess of the natives—interestingly they are referred to in a derogatory manner as *Brittunculi* (l. 5); and in *Tab.Vindol.* III.649 Britons are transporting an unknown cargo for Roman owners, *de carris Brittonum* (l. 2).
[57] Compare this view with that of A. Sargent, 'The North-South Divide Revisited: Thoughts on the Character of Roman Britain' in *Britannia*, Vol. 33 (2002), 224–26.
[58] Funari, 'The Consumption of Olive Oil.' p. 241.
[59] Funari, 'The Consumption of Olive Oil,' overall conclusion p. 262; and for market trade vs. redistribution pp. 244, 249.
[60] Erdkamp, 'The Corn Supply of the Roman Armies,' pp. 53–54; and Monfort, 'The Roman Military Supply,' pp. 75, 80.

locally as either taxes in kind, the purchase of grain at fixed prices, *frumentum emptum*, or through dealings with local and provincial traders.[61] Erdkamp's reason for stressing the role of the state in supply is his belief in Whittaker's 'theory of economic marginality' (as explained above), whilst Monfort claims that 'inadequate transport infrastructure and communication in Roman times' makes the hypothesis that there existed a market exchange mechanism extremely unlikely.[62]

However, although the existence of such an army supply system based on a highly developed and well-defined imperial organisation is not disproved by the Vindolanda Tablets, they do, on the other hand, impose some strict limits on the degree of coordination and control exercised by imperial authorities, as they bear witness to a command economy which was dynamic, flexible and operating in a grey zone between civilian and military, redistribution and the market.

Nor, moreover, is the basic assumption of some scholars that supply within a local context was impossible and could only be of a supplementary nature supported by the tablets. To be sure, they do not prove that grain supply was a purely local matter either, but they should give cause for thought: if one of the largest textual corpuses of its kind provides evidence of every kind of food, particularly grain, being bought and sold locally by civilians and soldiers alike, and gives no hint as to long-distance import or shortage of grain in general, then the possibility of a higher degree of regional self-sufficiency is worth taking into consideration—especially as concrete evidence of grain-taxes and an imperial supply-network administered by the *praefectus annonae* is more or less non-existent.[63]

These issues pertaining to the rather narrow study of the supply system of the Roman army have much wider implications when we relate them to the historiography of the economy of Roman Britain, as discussed in chapter two: what was the economic role and influence of the army? How early did the economy of the province begin to develop significantly? Why were there no villas in the northern highlands? And what kind of livelihood did the northern farmers pursue?

Once again, the Vindolanda Tablets provide no conclusive answers, but they do give some interesting pointers: first, although a large part of the overall command economy of the army may have been circumscribed by various measures, there is evidence of a thriving market economy at Vindolanda fuelled by the expenditure of salaries and the official purchase of necessary supplies made available locally, which, although conducted through middlemen, must have made cash flow from the army to native producers, thus stimulating the general economy of the province.[64] Second, and by implication, as the tablets date from *c.* AD 85–130, the economy of the province must have been rather highly developed as early as the turn of the 1st century AD in order to provide the range and scale of goods attested.[65]

Thirdly, claims that the northern highland zone was too thinly populated and barren to contribute to the food supply of the Roman garrisons along the frontier and that the basis for a 'villa economy' did therefore not exist should be reconsidered: if grain was actually traded freely, the reason is less likely to be the economic marginality of the land and overexploitation by the army, as the nature of native, highland society and the weak incentives for a local aristocracy to develop in an army-dominated area.[66] Finally, and as a direct consequence, the Vindolanda Tablets provide further evidence for the false dichotomy between lowland arable and highland pastoral farming—the tablets certainly attest to a plentiful supply of all kinds of meat, but they also attest to the growing of grain in a local context, both emmer, spelt and barley.[67]

However, in closing, what is truly significant about the Vindolanda Tablets is not the evidence they provide of economic structures as such, but about economic behaviour: although we may not be much wiser about the organisational intricacies of army supply,[68] we should certainly appreciate the insights provided into the ordinary, economic activities of a great number of Romans of different status, profession and origin. Throughout this study the tablets have been used to testify to the co-existence of three interdependent ways of institutionalising exchange within society, and it has been argued that we should not try to simplify their complex interaction: there was no single Vindolandan economy, but rather, different aspects of economic life were prominent in different contexts.

Accordingly, any attempt to fit the evidence of economic

---

[61] Erdkamp, 'The Corn Supply of the Roman Armies,' pp. 59–60, pp. 65–66 and p. 67, respectively; and Monfort, 'The Roman Military Supply,' pp. 72–73.
[62] Erdkamp, 'The Corn Supply of the Roman Armies,' p. 67; and Monfort, 'The Roman Military Supply,' p. 80.
[63] See Erdkamp, 'The Corn Supply of the Roman Armies,' pp. 59–60, who defends his interpretation by arguing *ex silentio*. See also Millett, *The Romanization of Britain*, pp. 56–57, who argues that the burden of food supply was not excessive.
[64] Supporting the views of Richmond, *Roman Britain*, p. 135; Frere, *Britannia*, pp. 217, 254, 281, 291; Wacher, *Roman Britain*, pp. 107, 141; Todd, *Roman Britain*, p. 110; and Salway, *Roman Britain*, pp. 235–38, 619–25.
[65] This has been the view of most authors since Collingwood, *Roman Britain*, p. 226; but for more recent, similar views, see Todd, *Roman Britain*, p. 111; and Millett, *The Romanization of Britain*, pp. 99, 123.
[66] As argued in different ways by Millet, *The Romanization of Britain*, pp. 94, 100–1, 120; Wacher, *Roman Britain*, pp. 134–35, 139; and Shotter, *Roman Britain*, pp. 77–78. Indeed, prior to the foundation of the first Vindolandan timber fort there is archaeological evidence of a native farming community in the area with finds of plough marks, farm steads, a possible religious tribal centre and a small hillfort; R. Birley, *A Roman Frontier Fort*, pp. 39–40. Moreover, according to J. Taylor, *An Atlas of Roman Rural Settlements in England*, CBA Research Report 151 (Oxford, 2007), p. 88, 'rural settlement in the vicinity of the Roman military communities along Hadrian's Wall was overwhelmingly focused on dispersed, enclosed farms.' See, likewise, *ibid.*, pp. 42–43, 57, 59.
[67] Proponents of comparable views are Richmond, *Roman Britain*, p. 132; Frere, *Britannia*, pp. 217, 260, 265; and Wacher, *A Portrait of Roman Britain*, p. 26.
[68] As Whittaker laments, 'Supplying the Army,' p. 233.

activity from Vindolanda into the 'traditional,' historiographical framework of studies of the ancient economy has highly ambiguous consequences: first of all, the large flow of goods employing various exchange mechanisms as well as the extensive cash economy evident at the fort are modernist traits; second, the potentially circumscribed nature of this exchange which is due to the army constituting such a small fraction of the population of the Empire could mean that we are missing out on the greater—primitivist—picture of an agrarian economy of self-sufficiency; third, the extensive market economy attested in the tablets as well as the 'economic rationality' inherent in producing accounts of economic activities which were based on redistribution and even reciprocity speaks strongly in the favour of formalism; and finally, it is equally evident that 'economic embeddedness' was also a factor and that we should be aware of the possible consequences of exchange based on reciprocity for the supply-mechanisms which it employed.

Hence, this study can only applaud recent works which stress the multiple—often overlapping and ambiguous—behaviours evident in ancient economic activity. The crux of the matter is that this is not an issue of the institution of the market versus either a political or socially embedded economy, but about the way in which these exchange mechanisms combine to form a complex system defined by the specific circumstances. This combination of mechanisms is one substantial reason why attempts to characterise the whole of the ancient economy as either primitivist, modernist, formalist or substantivist are misleading.[69]

Although it would be wrong to presume that the special conditions pertaining to a specific military community were representative of the Roman Empire at the time, the Vindolanda Tablets do provide ample ground for inference about that part of the wider economy which towered above the level of subsistence and self-sufficiency. Specifically, they have enabled us to glimpse an interrelationship between different uses of exchange mechanisms which implies that even though the Romans did not develop any theory of economics as such, they certainly possessed a culturally specific economic rationality which allowed them to operate within three different institutional frameworks and to distinguish effortlessly between them at a practical level.[70]

---

[69] As recently argued in different ways by Andreau, *Banking and Business*, p. 152–53; J. K. Davies, 'Hellenistic Economies in the Post-Finley Era,' in Z. Archibald, J. K. Davies, V. Gabrielsen and G. J. Oliver (eds), *Hellenistic Economies* (London and New York, 2001), p. 12; P. Cartledge, 'The Economy (Economies) of Ancient Greece,' in W. Scheidel and S. von Reden (eds), *The Ancient Economy* (Edinburgh, 2002), p. 13; I. Haynes, 'Britain's First Information Revolution. The Roman Army and the Transformation of Economic Life,' in P. Erdkamp (ed.), *The Roman Army and the Economy* (Amsterdam, 2002), p. 116; Z. Archibald, 'Markets and Exchange: The Structure and Scale of Economic Behaviour in the Hellenistic Age,' in Z. Archibald, J. K. Davies and V. Gabrielsen (eds), *Making, Moving and Managing: The New World of Ancient Economies, 323–31 BC* (Oxford, 2004), p. 3; and W. Scheidel, R. Saller and I. Morris, 'Introduction,' in W. Scheidel, R. Saller and I. Morris (eds), *The Cambridge Economic History of the Greco-Roman World* (Cambridge, 2007), pp. 11–12.

[70] Compare with Polanyi, 'Preface,' p. xvii; Finley, *The Ancient Economy*, pp. 21–23; Andreau, *Banking and Business*, p. 109; Cartledge, 'The Economy (Economies) of Ancient Greece,' p. 16; and Bang, *The Roman Bazaar*, p. 32.

Epilogue

This study has assessed the significance of the new evidence provided by the Vindolanda Tablets for our understanding of the economy of the early Roman Empire. The focus has been on analysing evidence of economic activities in terms of three different modes of exchange, and it has been argued that both the institution of the market, redistribution and reciprocity are all widely attested in different contexts at Vindolanda. More importantly, the significance of this finding does not lie merely in confirming the usefulness of these concepts for analysing the Roman economy, but in describing a system in which all three modes were active and prominent at the same time and thereby in unison constituted a multi-layered economic system.

Also, it has been possible to sketch tentatively a Roman economy in which even an outpost like Vindolanda was surprisingly well connected with the greater whole: all three layers of the multi-layered economy attested have been shown to have operated on both a local, provincial and imperial level, as the institution of the market merged with a wider political economy and an embedded economy specific to the military community of Vindolanda.

Furthermore, it has been argued that the evidence provided by the Vindolanda Tablets should affect our views on a number of more specific issues: first and foremost, Roman army supply and state redistribution in general should be considered more dynamic, flexible and integrated with the institution of the market; second, a higher degree of regional self-sufficiency should be considered in areas otherwise thought 'economically marginal;' and as concerns the economy of Roman Britain, the tablets favour interpretations suggesting that the army was an important stimulator of the economy of the province, that this economy was already quite developed by the 1st century AD, that the societies of the highland zone should be attributed more economic significance, and that they were by no means exclusively pastoral.

In summary, the most important achievement of this study has, I hope, been to underline the need for a more nuanced interpretation of the ancient economy. As a consequence, the economy of Vindolanda should be perceived as being constituted by three interdependent ways of institutionalising exchange within society, and hence, the resulting economic system displays multiple, ambiguous characteristics and behaviours which cannot readily be subsumed into a single, traditional model. Moreover, this implies that even though the Romans necessarily perceived economic matters in a different light than modern observers, the tablets provide ample evidence that they should not be considered economically naïve or ignorant, for although they organised their economy differently, the individuals encountered in the tablets display a high degree of economic rationality.

To be sure, Vindolanda represents only a tiny outpost in the Roman world, the fifty years covered by the Vindolanda Tablets are only a brief slice of ancient history, and this study comprises a single case-study based on a *corpus* of evidence that has to be interpreted with some caution; but it still has significant implications for our understanding of the ancient economy as a whole. Accordingly, it is fascinating to consider where further research might lead, for similar finds of Roman everyday records continue to be made—as illustrated by the analyses conducted in chapters three, four and five which were lent more weight by comparison with activities at *Luguvalium*, *Vindonissa*, Bu Njem, *Mons Claudianus* and *Dura-Europus*.

Therefore, future scholarly enquiries into the subject must include these and other comparable sources, for the more information about ancient economic activity we can glean from the available evidence, the better equipped we will be in our endeavours to model, explain and comprehend not only the ancient economy, but also key aspects of life in antiquity, such as social- and political organisation, living conditions, and cultural- and religious practices, to mention some of the more significant possibilities. In short, such studies can provide valuable new insights into parts of ancient society otherwise mostly known through the writings of its élites and the mute testimony of ruins, shipwrecks and pottery distribution-maps.

Appendix

During the course of my work on the original master's dissertation, it became evident at an early stage that a comprehensive, quantitative analysis of the economic activities attested by the Vindolanda Tablets would be highly useful.[1] Therefore, an Excel-database was constructed from which the present Appendix has been fashioned and which has provided the basic data for the wider analyses of this study. For the convenience of the reader, and so that it may be easier to obtain a quick grasp of the entire *corpus* of relevant evidence, a simplified version of this database is appended below.

Each discernible transaction has been described using the following categories:

- **Tablet number:** the official, *Tabulae Vindolandenses* reference numbers.

- **Period:** the time period to which each tablet is attributed, see p. 2.

- **Type of economic relation:** an attempt has been made to categorise each transaction, although some can only be labelled as belonging to some kind of account.

- **Commodity:** the type of good exchanged; for many textiles only the Latin name has been given, as there is no proper English translation available.

- **Quantities and prices:** if available and in Roman measures.

- **Supplier, seller or creditor:** the identity of the person supplying, selling or extending credit.

- **Receiver or payer:** the identity of receiver, buyer or debtor.

---

[1] As the database predates the publication of *Tab. Vindol.* IV.i, the twenty-six transactions attested in the latter are not included. However, seeing that the original analysis was based on the evidence of more than five hundred discernible transactions, the new data presents far too few transactions to alter the overall results—on the contrary, they fit the existing picture very well.

Appendix

Tab. Vindol.	Period	Type of transaction	Commodity	Quantity	Price	Supplier, seller or creditor	Receiver or payer
159	3	redistribution	barley-money			Army	Cavalry
178	3	redistribution	revenues of the fort		80 denarii	Army	Unknown
179	3	account	Unknown		274.5 denarii, 1 as	Unknown	Unknown
180	4	redistribution	wheat			"hominem transmarinum"	"hominem transmarinum"
180	4	redistribution	wheat	7 *modii*		"hominem transmarinum"	Macrinus
180	4	debt	wheat	26 *modii*		"hominem transmarinum"	Felicius Victor
180	4	redistribution	wheat	19 *modii*		"hominem transmarinum"	father of "hom. transm."
180	4	redistribution	wheat	13 *modii*		"hominem transmarinum"	Macrinus
180	4	redistribution	wheat	8 *modii*		"hominem transmarinum"	the oxherds at the wood
180	4	redistribution	wheat	3 *modii*		"hominem transmarinum"	Amabilis at the shrine
180	4	redistribution	wheat	3 *modii*		"hominem transmarinum"	Crescens
180	4	redistribution	wheat			"hominem transmarinum"	Unknown
180	4	redistribution	wheat	15 *modii*		"hominem transmarinum"	Macr...
180	4	redistribution	wheat			"hominem transmarinum"	Ma...
180	4	redistribution	wheat	2 *modii*		"hominem transmarinum"	father of "hom. transm."
180	4	redistribution	wheat	6 *modii*		"hominem transmarinum"	Lu... the beneficiarius
180	4	redistribution	wheat	15 *modii*		"hominem transmarinum"	Felicius Victor
180	4	redistribution	wheat	2 *modii*		"hominem transmarinum"	"you"
180	4	redistribution	wheat	9 *modii*		"hominem transmarinum"	Crescens
180	4	redistribution	wheat	11 *modii*		"hominem transmarinum"	legionary soldiers
180	4	redistribution	wheat			"hominem transmarinum"	Candidus
180	4	redistribution	wheat			"hominem transmarinum"	"you"
180	4	redistribution	wheat			"hominem transmarinum"	"you"
180	4	redistribution	wheat			"hominem transmarinum"	Lucco, in charge of the pigs
180	4	redistribution	wheat			"hominem transmarinum"	Primus, slave of Lucius
180	4	redistribution	wheat			"hominem transmarinum"	"you"

The Vindolanda Tablets and the Ancient Economy

Tab. Vindol.	Period	Type of transaction	Commodity	Quantity	Price	Supplier, seller or creditor	Receiver or payer
180	4	redistribution	wheat			"hominem transmarinum"	Lucco
180	4	redistribution	wheat			"hominem transmarinum"	Unknown
180	4	redistribution	wheat			"hominem transmarinum"	father, in charge of the oxen
180	4	redistribution	wheat			"hominem transmarinum"	"hominem transmarinum"
181	4	payment	sundries		2 *denarii*	"hominem transmarinum"	Candidus
181	4	payment	timber		7 *denarii*	"hominem transmarinum"	Candidus
181	4	payment	tunic	1	3 *denarii*	"hominem transmarinum"	Candidus
181	4	payment	Unknown			"hominem transmarinum"	Tetricus
181	4	payment	Unknown		2.5 *denarii*	"hominem transmarinum"	Primus
181	4	payment	Unknown		10 *denarii*	"hominem transmarinum"	Alio, the veterinary doctor
181	4	payment	Unknown		3 *denarii*	"hominem transmarinum"	Vitalis, the bath man
181	4	debt	Unknown		7 *denarii*	"hominem transmarinum"	Ingenuus
181	4	debt	Unknown		3 *denarii*	"hominem transmarinum"	Acranius
181	4	debt	Unknown		7 *denarii*	"hominem transmarinum"	Vardullian cavalrymen
181	4	debt	Unknown		3 *denarii*	"hominem transmarinum"	Companion of Tagamatis, the flag-bearer
182	4	payment	Unknown	15 *modii*	12 *denarii*, 3 *asses*	author 182	bugler
182	4	debt	sundries		2 *denarii*, 2 *asses*	author 182	bugler
182	4	payment	Unknown		38.5 *denarii*, 2 *asses*	author 182	Sabinus, from Trier
182	4	debt	bacon		13 *denarii*	author 182	Ircucisso
182	4	debt	bacon and bacon-lard	60.5 *pondii*	8 *denarii*, 2 *asses*	author 182	Felicio, the centurion
182	4	payment	sundries		6 *denarii*, 2 *asses*	Felicio, the centurion	author 182
182	4	debt	Unknown			author 182	Vattus
182	4	payment	horse	1		author 182	Victor
182	4	payment	Unknown			author 182	Exomnius, the centurion
182	4	debt	iron			author 182	Atrectus, the brewer

Appendix

Tab. Vindol.	Period	Type of transaction	Commodity	Quantity	Price	Supplier, seller or creditor	Receiver or payer
182	4	debt	pork-fat		11 *denarii*, 2 *asses*	author 182	Atrectus, the brewer
182	4	debt	Unknown			author 182	Andecarus
182	4	debt	Unknown			author 182	Sanctus
182	4	debt	Unknown		2 *denarii*, 1 *as*	author 182	...arius
182	4	debt	Unknown		2.5 *denarii*	author 182	Unknown
182	4	debt	Unknown		0.5 *denarius* 1.25 *asses*	author 182	Sautenus
182	4	debt	Unknown			author 182	Varia...
183	3	redistribution	iron	90 *pondii*		author 183	...tor, centurion
183	3	redistribution	Unknown		32 *denarii*	author 183	Ascanius
183	3	redistribution	Unknown			author 183	Candidus, in charge of the pigs
183	3	redistribution	Unknown			author 183	transporter
184	5	payment	overcoats		13 *denarii*	author 184	Tagarminis
184	5	payment	pepper		2 *denarii*	author 184	Gambax, son of Tappo
184	5	debt	towel	1	2 *denarii*	author 184	Sollemnis
184	5	payment	flask	1		author 184	Furio, son of Stipo
184	5	payment	towel	1	2 *denarii*	author 184	Ammius
184	5	debt	buskin		3.5 *denarii*	author 184	Messor
184	5	payment	*sagacia*	1	5 *denarii*, 6 *asses*	author 184	Lucius, the shield-maker
184	5	debt	tallow			author 184	Uxperus
184	5	debt	Unknown			author 184	Agilis?
184	5	debt	tallow			author 184	Huep...
184	5	debt	towel	1	2 *denarii*	author 184	Tullio, son of Carpentarius
184	5	debt	thongs		2.5 *denarii*	author 184	Butimas
184	5	payment	tallow		2 *denarii*	author 184	Butimas
184	5	debt	towel	1	1 *denarius*	author 184	Butimas
184	5	debt	tallow		2 *denarii*, 2 *asses*	author 184	Caledus

Tab. Vindol.	Period	Type of transaction	Commodity	Quantity	Price	Supplier, seller or creditor	Receiver or payer
184	5	debt	towel			author 184	Caledus
184	5	debt	tallow		2.5 *denarii*	author 184	Caledus
185	2	payment	lees of wine		0.5 *denarius*	Unknown	author 185
185	2	payment	lees of wine		0.25 *denarius*	Unknown	author 185
185	2	payment	lees of wine		0.25 *denarius*	Unknown	author 185
185	2	payment	lees of wine		0.125 *denarius*	Unknown	author 185
185	2	payment	barley	1 *modius*	0.5 *denarius*	Unknown	author 185
185	2	payment	wagon axles	2	3.5 *denarii*	Unknown	author 185
185	2	payment	salt and fodder		1 *denarius*	Unknown	author 185
185	2	payment	lees of wine		0.25 *denarius*	Unknown	author 185
185	2	payment	accommo-dation		0.5 *denarius*	Unknown	author 185
185	2	payment	lees of wine		0.25 *denarius*	Unknown	author 185
185	2	payment	vests		0.25 *denarius*	Unknown	author 185
185	2	payment	wheat	1 *modius*		Unknown	author 185
186	4	payment	Unknown	30 *modii*		Gracilis	author 186
186	4	payment	Unknown	100 *pondii*		Gracilis	author 186
186	4	payment	Unknown	22 *pondii*		Gracilis	author 186
186	4	payment	nails	100	2 *asses*	author 186	Gracilis
186	4	payment	salt	85 *pondii*	12 *asses*	Audax	author 186
186	4	payment	Celtic beer	6.25 *modii*	8 *asses*	Unknown	author 186
186	4	payment	goat-meat		1 *as*	Audax	author 186
186	4	payment	Unknown			Gracilis	author 186
186	4	payment	pork			Gracilis	author 186
186	4	payment	pork	11 *pondii*		Audax	author 186
186	4	payment	Celtic beer	6.25 *modii*		Similis	author 186
186	4	payment	Unknown			Audax	author 186
187	3	account	Unknown		0.25 *denarius*	author 187	Crispa, daughter/wife of Pollio

Appendix

Tab. Vindol.	Period	Type of transaction	Commodity	Quantity	Price	Supplier, seller or creditor	Receiver or payer
187	3	account	Unknown		0.5 denarius 1 as	author 187	Ingenuus, the veteran
190	3	reciprocity	Unknown	3 *modii*	0.5 *denarius*	author 190	Unknown
190	3	reciprocity	Unknown		0.5 *denarius*	author 190	Unknown
190	3	reciprocity	Unknown			author 190	festival
190	3	reciprocity	Unknown			author 190	festival
190	3	reciprocity	Unknown			author 190	festival
190	3	reciprocity	barley			author 190	Unknown
190	3	reciprocity	Celtic beer			author 190	Unknown
190	3	reciprocity	barley	4 *modii*		author 190	Unknown
190	3	reciprocity	Celtic beer	2 *modii*		author 190	Unknown
190	3	reciprocity	Unknown			author 190	The granary
190	3	reciprocity	Unknown	2 *modii*		author 190	Unknown
190	3	reciprocity	barley	5.5 *modii*		author 190	Unknown
190	3	reciprocity	wine, Massic			author 190	Allatus
190	3	reciprocity	barley	5.5 *modii*		author 190	Unknown
190	3	reciprocity	wine	1.88 *modii*		author 190	Unknown
190	3	reciprocity	Celtic beer	3 *modii*		author 190	Unknown
190	3	reciprocity	barley	6 *modii*		author 190	Unknown
190	3	reciprocity	Celtic beer	3 *modii*		author 190	Unknown
190	3	reciprocity	wine	1.75 *modii*		author 190	Unknown
190	3	reciprocity	sour wine	0.13 *modius*		Privatus	Unknown
190	3	reciprocity	fish-sauce	0.1 *modius*		Privatus	Unknown
190	3	reciprocity	pork-fat	0.63 *modius*		Privatus	the lord for charitable donations
190	3	reciprocity	wine	1 *modius*		author 190	festival
190	3	reciprocity	wine	0.75 *modius*		Privatus	Unknown
190	3	reciprocity	barley	0.72 *modius*		author 190	Unknown

The Vindolanda Tablets and the Ancient Economy

Tab. Vindol.	Period	Type of transaction	Commodity	Quantity	Price	Supplier, seller or creditor	Receiver or payer
191	3	account, domestic	spices			Unknown	? author 191/194/195/196/197
191	3	account, domestic	roe-deer			Unknown	? author 191/194/195/196/197
191	3	account, domestic	salt			Unknown	? author 191/194/195/196/197
191	3	account, domestic	pig, young			Unknown	? author 191/194/195/196/197
191	3	account, domestic	ham			Unknown	? author 191/194/195/196/197
191	3	account, domestic	wheat			Unknown	? author 191/194/195/196/197
191	3	account, domestic	venison			Unknown	? author 191/194/195/196/197
191	3	account, domestic	pickling			Unknown	? author 191/194/195/196/197
191	3	account, domestic	roe-deer			Unknown	? author 191/194/195/196/197
191	3	account, domestic	emmer			Unknown	? author 191/194/195/196/197
192	3	payment	coverlet	1		Gavo	author 192
192	3	payment	beans	55 *modii*		Gavo	author 192
192	3	payment	wool	38 *pondii*	27 *denarii*, 5 *asses*	Gavo	author 192
192	3	payment	Unknown		12.5 *denarii*, 1 *as*	Gavo	author 192
192	3	payment	bedspread	3		Gavo	author 192
192	3	payment	honey			Gavo	author 192
192	3	payment	*sagum*			Gavo	author 192
193	3	reciprocity	spices	0.03 *modius*	0.5 *denarius*	Unknown	Felicio, the centurion
193	3	reciprocity	gruel	0.03 *modius*	0,25 *denarius* 3 *asses*	Unknown	Felicio, the centurion
193	3	reciprocity	eggs	8	0.25 *denarius*	Unknown	Felicio, the centurion
194	3	account, domestic	shallow dishes	2		? author 191/194/195/196/197	Unknown
194	3	account, domestic	side-plates	5		? author 191/194/195/196/197	Unknown
194	3	account, domestic	vinegar-bowls			? author 191/194/195/196/197	Unknown
194	3	account, domestic	egg-cups	3		? author 191/194/195/196/197	Unknown
194	3	account, domestic	platter	1		? author 191/194/195/196/197	Unknown
194	3	account, domestic	shallow dish	1		? author 191/194/195/196/197	Unknown

Appendix

Tab. Vindol.	Period	Type of transaction	Commodity	Quantity	Price	Supplier, seller or creditor	Receiver or payer
194	3	account, domestic	strong-box?			? author 191/194/195/196/197	Unknown
194	3	account, domestic	bronze lamp			? author 191/194/195/196/197	Unknown
194	3	account, domestic	bread-baskets	4		? author 191/194/195/196/197	Unknown
194	3	account, domestic	cups	2		? author 191/194/195/196/197	Unknown
194	3	account, domestic	bowls	2		? author 191/194/195/196/197	Unknown
195	3	account, domestic	tunic	1		? author 191/194/195/196/197	Unknown
195	3	account, domestic	*abolla*	1		? author 191/194/195/196/197	Unknown
195	3	account, domestic	*abolla*	1		? author 191/194/195/196/197	Unknown
195	3	account, domestic	knife	1		? author 191/194/195/196/197	Unknown
196	3	account, domestic	blankets, pairs			? author 191/194/195/196/197	Unknown
196	3	account, domestic	*paenulae*, white			? author 191/194/195/196/197	Unknown
196	3	account, domestic	*paenulae*			? author 191/194/195/196/197	Unknown
196	3	account, domestic	*laena*			? author 191/194/195/196/197	Unknown
196	3	account, domestic	loose robe			? author 191/194/195/196/197	Unknown
196	3	account, domestic	*paenula*, under-			? author 191/194/195/196/197	Unknown
196	3	account, domestic	vests			Tranquilius	Unknown
196	3	account, domestic	*paenula*, under-			Tranquilius	Unknown
196	3	account, domestic	tunics, half-belted			? author 191/194/195/196/197	Unknown
196	3	account, domestic	tunics, for dining			? author 191/194/195/196/197	Unknown
196	3	account, domestic	branches			? author 191/194/195/196/197	Unknown
196	3	account, domestic	vase			? author 191/194/195/196/197	Unknown
196	3	account, domestic	rings			? author 191/194/195/196/197	Unknown
197	3	account	shoes			? author 191/194/195/196/197	Unknown
197	3	account	gallic shoes			? author 191/194/195/196/197	Unknown
201	2	account	flask			author 201	Unknown
202	2	account	fish-sauce			author 202	Unknown
203	4	account, domestic	pork-cutlet			author 203	Unknown

Tab. Vindol.	Period	Type of transaction	Commodity	Quantity	Price	Supplier, seller or creditor	Receiver or payer
203	4	account, domestic	bread-baskets			author 203	Unknown
203	4	account, domestic	wine	0.06 *modius*		author 203	Unknown
203	4	account, domestic	oil			author 203	Unknown
204	3	account	beans			author 204	Unknown
204	3	account	lentils			author 204	Unknown
204	3	account	lovage (spice)			author 204	Unknown
204	3	account	meal	10.5 *modii*		author 204	Unknown
205	4	account	Unknown			author 205	Unknown
206	3	payment	Unknown			author 206	Unknown
206	3	debt	Unknown			author 206	Unknown
207	3	account	*saga*	3		Gavo	Unknown
207	3	account	*sagacia*	7		Gavo	Unknown
207	3	account	Unknown	5		Gavo	Unknown
207	3	account	Unknown	15		Gavo	Unknown
207	3	account	capes			Gavo	Unknown
207	3	account	tunic	1		Gavo	Unknown
207	3	account	*palliola*	7		Gavo	Unknown
207	3	account	tunic	5		Marcus	Unknown
207	3	account	*palliola*	10		Marcus	Unknown
207	3	account	tunic	2		Marcus	Unknown
208	3	account	small dish			Praetorium slave	Unknown
208	3	account	*alliatum* (garlic paste)			Praetorium slave	Unknown
208	3	account	*conditum* (pickling)			Praetorium slave	Unknown
213	2	payment	barley			Cassius Saecularis	Natives
215	4	redistribution	wood			Severinus	*cornicularius*
215	4	redistribution	timber			Severinus	*cornicularius*
233	3	account	gruel			Praetorium slave	Unknown

Appendix

Tab. Vindol.	Period	Type of transaction	Commodity	Quantity	Price	Supplier, seller or creditor	Receiver or payer
233	3	account	pork-crackling			Praetorium slave	Unknown
233	3	account	trotters			Praetorium slave	Unknown
233	3	reciprocity	hunting-nets			Brocchus	Flavius Cerialis
234	3	redistribution	goods			Flavius Cerealis	Caecilius September
242	3	redistribution	pay			Flavius Cerealis	Felicio, the centurion
255	3	reciprocity	*sagacia*	6		Flavius Cerealis	Clodius Super, centurion
255	3	reciprocity	*saga*			Flavius Cerealis	Clodius Super, centurion
255	3	reciprocity	*palliola*	7		Flavius Cerealis	Clodius Super, centurion
255	3	reciprocity	tunics	6		Flavius Cerealis	Clodius Super, centurion
258	3	redistribution	bridge			Centurion	Flavius Cerialis
265	3	reciprocity	Sacrifice			Unknown	The day of the Kalends
299	5	reciprocity	oysters	50		Unknown	Unknown
301	2	payment	Unknown		5 *asses*	Unknown	Candidus, slave of Genialis the Prefect
301	2	payment	radishes		0.5 *denarius*	Unknown	Candidus, slave of Genialis the Prefect
302	1	payment	beans, bruised	2 *modii*		Unknown	Slave of Verecundus
302	1	payment	chickens	20		Unknown	Slave of Verecundus
302	1	payment	apples	100		Unknown	Slave of Verecundus
302	1	payment	eggs	150		Unknown	Slave of Verecundus
302	1	payment	fish-sauce	0.5 *modius*		Unknown	Slave of Verecundus
302	1	payment	olives	1 *modius*		Unknown	Slave of Verecundus
309	3	redistribution	hubs	34		Metto	Advectus
309	3	redistribution	axles for carts	38		Metto	Advectus
309	3	redistribution	axle turned on lathe	1		Metto	Advectus
309	3	redistribution	spokes	300		Metto	Advectus
309	3	redistribution	planks for a bed	26		Metto	Advectus
309	3	redistribution	seats	8		Metto	Advectus
309	3	redistribution	knots	2		Metto	Advectus

Tab. Vindol.	Period	Type of transaction	Commodity	Quantity	Price	Supplier, seller or creditor	Receiver or payer
309	3	redistribution	boards	20		Metto	Advectus
309	3	redistribution	Unknown	29		Metto	Advectus
309	3	redistribution	benches	6		Metto	Advectus
309	3	redistribution	goat-skins	6		Metto	Advectus
310	3	payment	pair of shears	1		Virilis, the veterinary doctor	Chrauttius
314	3	redistribution	lime			Unknown	Unknown
315	3	redistribution	wagons			Unknown	Unknown
316	3	redistribution	wagons			Unknown	Unknown
327	3	Unknown	*aes minutum*			Unknown	Unknown
343	4	Unknown	sinew	100 *pondii*		Marius	Octavius
343	4	payment	grain (*spica*)	5000 *modii*	800 *denarii*	Unknown	Octavius
343	4	reciprocity	hides			Candidus	Octavius
343	4	debt	*denarii*		8.5 *denarii*	Octavius	Tertius
343	4	account	hides	170		Octavius	Unknown
343	4	account	emmer (*bracis*)	119 *modii*		Octavius	Unknown
346	4	reciprocity	Socks, pairs from Satua			author 346/655	Unknown
346	4	reciprocity	sandals, pairs	2		author 346/655	Unknown
346	4	reciprocity	underpants, pairs	2		author 346/655	Unknown
346	4	reciprocity	sandals, pairs	2		author 346/655	Unknown
348	4	payment	emmer (*bracis*)			author 346/655	Unknown
581	3	account, domestic	Celtic beer			Author 581	Decurions
581	3	account, domestic	Unknown			Author 581	the brewer
581	3	account, domestic	chickens			Author 581	Unknown
581	3	account, domestic	Unknown			Author 581	Crescens
581	3	account, domestic	goose	1		Author 581	Unknown
581	3	account, domestic	Unknown			Author 581	Suetius
581	3	account, domestic	Unknown			Author 581	the brewer

Appendix

Tab. Vindol.	Period	Type of transaction	Commodity	Quantity	Price	Supplier, seller or creditor	Receiver or payer
581	3	account, domestic	Unknown			Author 581	Vatto
581	3	account, domestic	chickens			Author 581	Veterans
581	3	account, domestic	Unknown			Author 581	Sautenus
581	3	account, domestic	Unknown			Author 581	Chnisso
581	3	account, domestic	chickens			Author 581	Unknown
581	3	account, domestic	Unknown			Author 581	Ma...
581	3	account, domestic	Unknown			Author 581	Candidus
581	3	account, domestic	Unknown			Author 581	Mar...
581	3	account, domestic	Unknown			Author 581	Exsomnius
581	3	account, domestic	geese			Author 581	V... in charge of draft-animals of Brocchus
581	3	account, domestic	geese			Author 581	Unknown
581	3	account, domestic	chickens, nurselings			Author 581	Unknown
581	3	account, domestic	nurselings			Author 581	Unknown
581	3	account, domestic	chickens			Author 581	Unknown
581	3	account, domestic	chickens			Comm...	Unknown
581	3	account, domestic	chickens			Author 581	Unknown
581	3	reciprocity	chicken			Author 581	Unknown
581	3	reciprocity	chicken			Author 581	Unknown
581	3	reciprocity	chicken			Author 581	Unknown
581	3	reciprocity	Unknown			Author 581	Legate
581	3	reciprocity	Unknown			Author 581	Unknown
581	3	reciprocity	Unknown			Author 581	Flavius' discharge
581	3	reciprocity	Unknown			Author 581	Niger and Broccus
581	3	reciprocity	Unknown			Author 581	Brocchus' dinner
581	3	reciprocity	Unknown			Author 581	Brocchus
581	3	reciprocity	Unknown			Author 581	The lords at Matronalia
581	3	reciprocity	Unknown			Author 581	Niger and Lae...

Tab. Vindol.	Period	Type of transaction	Commodity	Quantity	Price	Supplier, seller or creditor	Receiver or payer
581	3	reciprocity	Unknown			Author 581	Brocchus
581	3	reciprocity	Unknown			Author 581	September
581	3	reciprocity	Unknown			Author 581	Sautenus
581	3	reciprocity	Unknown			Author 581	Unknown
581	3	reciprocity	geese			Author 581	Unknown
581	3	reciprocity	Unknown			Author 581	Onesimus, with the standards
581	3	reciprocity	Unknown			Author 581	Sautenus
581	3	reciprocity	Unknown			Author 581	as lunch for…
581	3	reciprocity	Unknown			Author 581	Flavinus
581	3	reciprocity	Unknown			Author 581	Sautenus
581	3	reciprocity	Unknown			Author 581	lunch with the governor
581	3	reciprocity	Unknown			Author 581	Myr… outside the camp
581	3	reciprocity	chickens	4		Author 581	Unknown
581	3	reciprocity	Unknown	12		Surenus the centurion	Unknown
581	3	reciprocity	chickens			Author 581	Unknown
581	3	reciprocity	chickens			Author 581	Sautenus
581	3	reciprocity	chickens	20		Author 581	Unknown
581	3	reciprocity	chickens, Tanagrian			Author 581	Unknown
581	3	reciprocity	chickens, sterile			Author 581	Unknown
581	3	reciprocity	chickens			Author 581	Unknown
582	3	account	chickens		10 denarii	Chnisso	Unknown
582	3	reciprocity	chickens	10		Chnisso	Prefect
582	3	account	Unknown		5.5 denarii, 1 as	Unknown	Unknown
582	3	account	chickens	8		Author 582	Unknown
582	3	account, domestic	chickens	21	9.5 denarii, 1 as	Author 582	Unknown
583	3	redistribution	wagons			Unknown	Unknown

Appendix

Tab. Vindol.	Period	Type of transaction	Commodity	Quantity	Price	Supplier, seller or creditor	Receiver or payer
584	3	redistribution	wagons			Unknown	Unknown
585	3	redistribution	wagons			Unknown	Unknown
586	3	reciprocity	*siliginis* (soft wheat)	2 *modii*		Author 586	Unknown
586	3	reciprocity	*halicae* (gruel)	1 *modius*		Author 586	Unknown
586	3	reciprocity	*halicae* (gruel)	1 *modius*		Author 586	Atticus, *cornicularis*
586	3	reciprocity	*siliginis* (soft wheat)	1 *modius*		Author 586	Atticus, *cornicularis*
586	3	reciprocity	*halicae* (gruel)	5 *modii*		Author 586	Vitalis, pharmacist
586	3	reciprocity	*siliginis* (soft wheat)	1 *modius*		Author 586	Vitalis, pharmacist
586	3	reciprocity	*siliginis* (soft wheat)	1 *modius*		Author 586	Decimus, *cornicularis*
586	3	reciprocity	Unknown	1 *modius*		Author 586	Unknown
586	3	reciprocity	*siliginis* (soft wheat)	50 *modii*		Unknown	Unknown
586	3	reciprocity	*siliginis* (soft wheat)			Masclus, the decurion	Author 586
586	3	reciprocity	*siliginis* (soft wheat)			Vitalis	Author 586
586	3	reciprocity	*siliginis* (soft wheat)	1 *modius*		Masclus, the decurion	Author 586
587	3	account	pork	1		Varius	Unknown
587	3	account	pork			Analeugus	Unknown
588	3	payment	cooking bowls			Adiutor	Unknown
588	3	payment	mustard-seed			Adiutor	Unknown
588	3	payment	anise	0.06 *modius*	0.25 *denarius*	Adiutor	Unknown
588	3	payment	caraway	0.03 *modius*	0.125 *denarius*	Adiutor	Unknown
588	3	payment	thyme	0.06 *modius*	0.125 *denarius*	Adiutor	Unknown
588	3	payment	Unknown			Adiutor	Unknown
589	4	account	oil			Unknown	Amabilis
589	4	account	oil			Unknown	Unknown
589	4	account	flask			Unknown	Amabilis
590	Uncertain	account	glass vessel			Cook	Audax
590	Uncertain	account	cooking-pot			Cook	…urius

The Vindolanda Tablets and the Ancient Economy

Tab. Vindol.	Period	Type of transaction	Commodity	Quantity	Price	Supplier, seller or creditor	Receiver or payer
590	Uncertain	account	glass vessel			Cook	… of Firmanus
590	Uncertain	account	glass vessel			Cook	…ns, decurion
590	Uncertain	account	dish			Cook	Unknown
590	Uncertain	account	glass vessel			Cook	Unknown
590	Uncertain	account	scale			Cook	Unknown
591	3	account	anise			Unknown	Unknown
591	3	account	nuts			Unknown	Unknown
591	3	account	berries			Unknown	Unknown
591	3	account	*siliginis* (soft wheat)			Unknown	Unknown
591	3	account	beans			Unknown	Unknown
591	3	account	alum			Unknown	Unknown
591	3	account	wax			Unknown	Unknown
591	3	account	bitumen			Unknown	Unknown
591	3	account	glue, bull's			Unknown	Unknown
591	3	account	pitch			Unknown	Unknown
591	3	account	blacking			Unknown	Unknown
591	3	account	anchusa			Unknown	Unknown
591	3	account	mustard-seed			Unknown	Unknown
591	3	account	verdigris			Unknown	Unknown
591	3	account	linen, soaked in honey			Unknown	Unknown
591	3	account	resin			Unknown	Unknown
591	3	account	cummin			Unknown	Unknown
591	3	account	oak-gall			Unknown	Unknown
592	3	account	honey			Unknown	Unknown
592	3	account	beet			Unknown	Unknown
592	3	account	ointment			Unknown	Unknown
592	3	account	eggs			Unknown	Unknown

Appendix

Tab. Vindol.	Period	Type of transaction	Commodity	Quantity	Price	Supplier, seller or creditor	Receiver or payer
592	3	account	sandals, pairs			Unknown	Unknown
592	3	account	cooking-pot			Unknown	Unknown
592	3	account	beef			Unknown	Unknown
592	3	account	pasta			Unknown	Unknown
593	3	account	net, for thrushes	1		Unknown	Unknown
593	3	account	net, for ducks	1		Unknown	Unknown
593	3	account	net, -drag, for fish	1		Unknown	Unknown
593	3	account	snares, for swans	3		Unknown	Unknown
593	3	account	snares	7		Unknown	Veteranus
594	3	account	*segosi* (hunting-dogs)			Unknown	Veteranus
594	3	account	*vertragi* (hunting-dogs)			Unknown	Veteranus
596	3	account, domestic	necklace-locks	2	7.25 *denarii*	author 596	Unknown
596	3	account, domestic	cloacks	6	69 *denarii*	author 596	Unknown
596	3	account, domestic	headbands	5	3.75 *denarii*	author 596	Unknown
596	3	account, domestic	hair	9 *pondii*	51.75 *denarii*	author 596	Unknown
596	3	account, domestic	drawers	10	25 *denarii*	author 596	Unknown
596	3	account, domestic	saddle	1	12 *denarii*	author 596	Unknown
596	3	account, domestic	cloaks, of bark	15	236 *denarii*	author 596	Unknown
596	3	account, domestic	bags	10	6.875 *denarii*	author 596	Unknown
596	3	account, domestic	bowls	4	20.25 *denarii*	author 596	Unknown
596	3	account, domestic	bowls	4	15.75 *denarii*	author 596	Unknown
596	3	account, domestic	bowls	4	10.75 *denarii*	author 596	Unknown
596	3	account, domestic	reins	2	7 *denarii*	author 596	Unknown
596	3	account, domestic	curtain, scarlet	1	54.63 *denarii*	author 596	Unknown
596	3	account, domestic	curtain, greenish-yellow	1	46.75 *denarii*	author 596	Unknown
596	3	account, domestic	curtain, purple	2	99.63 *denarii*	author 596	Unknown

Tab. Vindol.	Period	Type of transaction	Commodity	Quantity	Price	Supplier, seller or creditor	Receiver or payer
596	3	account, domestic	curtain	1	55.13 *denarii*	author 596	Unknown
597	3	redistribution	bolt, for bread-box	1		author 597	Unknown
597	3	redistribution	pots, repaired	2		author 597	Unknown
597	3	redistribution	dog-collars			author 597	Unknown
597	3	redistribution	bolt	1		author 597	Unknown
597	3	redistribution	yoke of a suspended carriage			author 597	Unknown
598	3	account	yoke of a suspended carriage			author 598	Unknown
599	3	redistribution	bronze	5 *pondii*		author 599	Taurinus
599	3	redistribution	lanterns			author 599	M…
599	3	redistribution	nails for a suspended chariot			author 599	Unknown
600	5	redistribution	seats			author 600	Unknown
600	5	redistribution	felloes	4		author 600	Unknown
600	5	redistribution	timbers for covering			author 600	Unknown
600	5	redistribution	curved ribs	4		author 600	Unknown
600	5	redistribution	board for body of carriage			author 600	Unknown
601	3	account	Unknown			Unknown	Florus
601	3	account	Unknown			Unknown	Modestinus
601	3	account	nails			Unknown	Florus
601	3	account	Unknown			Unknown	Florus
601	3	account	Unknown			Florus	Unknown
601	3	account	pork-fat			Unknown	Unknown
601	3	account	Unknown			Unknown	Florus
601	3	account	nails			Unknown	Florus
601	3	account	Unknown			Unknown	Vitalis
602	3	account	gallic shoes			Unknown	Unknown
602	3	account	gallic shoes			Unknown	Unknown

Appendix

Tab. Vindol.	Period	Type of transaction	Commodity	Quantity	Price	Supplier, seller or creditor	Receiver or payer
603	3	redistribution	nails			author 603	Unknown
603	3	redistribution	nails			author 603	sandals of Renatus
603	3	redistribution	nails	20		author 603	shoes of Taurus
603	3	redistribution	nails			author 603	boots of Florenti…
603	3	redistribution	nails	26		author 603	Unknown
603	3	redistribution	nails			author 603	Unknown
603	3	redistribution	nails			author 603	Arcanus in respect of the shoes (?)
603	3	redistribution	nails			author 603	Unknown
604	3	payment	nails	350		Taurinus	author 604
604	3	redistribution	nails	25		author 604/607	sandals of Tetricus
604	3	redistribution	nails	20		author 604/607	shoes of …a
604	3	redistribution	nails	30		author 604/607	boots of Prudentius
605	3	redistribution	nails	12		author 605	shoes of Lucanus
605	3	redistribution	nails	9		author 605	shoes of Taurinus
605	3	redistribution	nails	11		author 605	shoes of Aventinus
605	3	redistribution	nails	11		author 605	Unknown
607	3	payment	yarn		0.25 *denarius* 1 *as*	Taurinus	author 604/607
607	3	redistribution	yarn			author 604/607	cloak of Aventinus
607	3	redistribution	money-belt			author 604/607	money-belt of Lucanus
607	3	redistribution	shirt			author 604/607	shirt of Crescens
608	Uncertain	account	clothing			Unknown	Belli.e..
608	Uncertain	account	clothing			Gami.oni	Unknown
608	Uncertain	account	clothing			Sollemnis	Unknown
608	Uncertain	account	clothing			Crescens	Unknown
608	Uncertain	account	clothing			Felici	Unknown
608	Uncertain	account	clothing			Victor	Unknown

Tab. Vindol.	Period	Type of transaction	Commodity	Quantity	Price	Supplier, seller or creditor	Receiver or payer
608	Uncertain	account	clothing			Unknown	Scorvilo
608	Uncertain	account	clothing			Fidelis	Unknown
608	Uncertain	account	clothing			Germanus	Unknown
608	Uncertain	account	clothing			Valenti..	Unknown
609	2	debt	Unknown		2.5 *denarii*	Veruinius	Unknown
609	2	debt	Unknown		2.5 *denarii*	Veruinius	Unknown
609	2	debt	Unknown		0.5 *denarius*	Veruinius	Unknown
609	2	debt	Unknown		1 *denarius*	Veruinius	Unknown
609	2	debt	Unknown		2 *denarii*	Veruinius	Unknown
609	2	debt	Unknown			Veruinius	.s.o
609	2	debt	Unknown			Veruinius	…aria…
609	2	debt	Unknown			Veruinius	Frissi.
609	2	debt	Unknown			Veruinius	Suasso
609	2	debt	Unknown			Veruinius	Germanus
609	2	debt	Unknown			Veruinius	Ca.ussa
609	2	debt	Unknown			Veruinius	Marcellinus
609	2	debt	Unknown			Veruinius	Modius
609	2	debt	Unknown			Veruinius	Senecio
609	2	debt	Unknown			Veruinius	Sactius
609	2	debt	Unknown			Veruinius	Viator
609	2	debt	Unknown			Veruinius	Crescens
609	2	debt	Unknown			Veruinius	Crenscens
609	2	debt	Unknown			Veruinius	Leubius
609	2	debt	Unknown			Veruinius	Varienus
611	Uncertain	debt	Unknown			Unknown	Unknown
615	3	payment	*vectura*			Huntsmen	Unknown
616	3	account	chickens	2		Unknown	Unknown

Appendix

Tab. Vindol.	Period	Type of transaction	Commodity	Quantity	Price	Supplier, seller or creditor	Receiver or payer
628	3	redistribution	Celtic beer			Flavius Cerialis, prefect	Masclus
632	Uncertain	redistribution	accommo-dation			Unknown	Flavius Cerialis...
641	3	reciprocity	bronze lamp, small	1		Arcanus	Marinus
642	4	reciprocity	shingles	100		Bellicus	Gabinius
643	3	reciprocity	axe	1		Titus	Florus
643	3	reciprocity	small box	1		Calavirus	*Beneficiarius*
645	3	payment	emmer (*bracis*)			Maior	Cocceiius Maritimus
646	2	payment	Unknown			Optatus, the maltster	Montanus
647	4	debt	forfeited property			Unknown	Unknown
648	Uncertain	debt	Unknown			Suolcenus	Candidus
649	2	redistribution	emmer (*bracis*)	381 *modii*		Rac..romaucus	...nus
649	2	payment	*velatura*			Unknown	Britons
649	2	payment	*vectura*			...nus	Britons
649	2	payment	Unknown			Unknown	...nus
650	2	debt	*denarii*			Ascanius, *comes Augusti*	surveyor
655	3	reciprocity	*denarii*			Unknown	Unknown
661	3	reciprocity	gift			Unknown	Unknown
672	4	account	*membranum* (skin/ parchment)			Unknown	Unknown
672	4	account	*bucculam* (helmet cheek-piece)			Unknown	Unknown
673	Uncertain	account	*siliginis* (soft wheat)			Unknown	Unknown
673	Uncertain	account	sour wine			Unknown	Unknown
675	3	account	radish			Unknown	Unknown
677	3	account	dog, puppy			Unknown	Unknown
678	3	account	Unknown	0.25 *modius*	0.75 *denarius*	Unknown	Unknown
678	3	account	Unknown	2 *pondii*		Unknown	Unknown
678	3	account	Unknown	0.5 *pondius*	0.5 *denarius*	Unknown	Unknown

The Vindolanda Tablets and the Ancient Economy

Tab. Vindol.	Period	Type of transaction	Commodity	Quantity	Price	Supplier, seller or creditor	Receiver or payer
678	3	account	Unknown	0.03 *modius*	0.5 *denarius*	Unknown	Unknown
679	3	account	chicken	1		Unknown	Unknown
679	3	account	olives			Unknown	Unknown
684	3	account	timber, beams			Unknown	for a granary

Bibliography

Primary sources:

Bingen, J., *et al*. (eds), *Mons Claudianus. Ostraca Graeca et Latina*, vols. I–IV (Cairo, 1992–2009).

Bowman, A. K. and J. D. Thomas (eds), *Vindolanda: the Latin Writing–Tablets (Tabulae Vindolandenses I)*, Britannia Monograph Series No. 4 (London, 1983).

Bowman, A. K. and J. D. Thomas (eds), *The Vindolanda Writing–Tablets (Tabulae Vindolandenses II)* (London, 1994).

Bowman, A. K. and J. D. Thomas (eds), *The Vindolanda Writing–Tablets (Tabulae Vindolandenses III)* (London, 2003).

Bowman, A. K., J. D. Thomas and R. S. O. Tomlin (eds), 'The Vindolanda Writing-Tablets (*Tabulae Vindolandenses IV, Part 1*),' in *Britannia*, 41 (2010), 187–224.

Caesar, J., *Bellum Gallicum* in *The Gallic War*, The Loeb Classical Library (London and New York, 1922).

Collingwood, R. G. and R. P. Wright (eds), *Roman Inscriptions in Britain*, *RIB* I (Oxford, 1965).

Frere, S. S., (ed.), *The Roman Inscriptions of Britain*, *RIB* II (Stroud, 1995).

Marichal, R., (ed.), *Les Ostraca de Bu Njem* (Tripoli, 1992).

Petrie, H., and J. Sharpe (eds), *Monumenta Historica Britannica* (London, 1848).

Speidel, M. A., (ed.), *Die römischen Schreibtafeln von Vindonissa* (Brugg, 1996).

Strabo, *Geographica* in *The Geography of Strabo*, The Loeb Classical Library (Cambridge, MA; and London, 1917–32).

Tacitus, C., *Agricola* in *Agricola; Germania; Dialogus*, The Loeb Classical Library, rev. edn (London, 1970).

Tacitus, C., *Germania* in *Agricola; Germania; Dialogus*, The Loeb Classical Library, rev. edn (London, 1970).

Tacitus, C., *Historiae* in *The Histories*, The Loeb Classical Library (London, 1931–37).

Tomlin, R. S. O., (ed.), 'Roman Manuscripts from Carlisle: The Ink-Written Tablets' in *Britannia*, 29 (1998), 31–84.

Welles, C. B., *et al*. (eds), *The Excavations at Dura-Europus, Final Report V, Part I: The Parchments and Papyri* (New Haven, 1959).

Secondary sources:

Andreau, J., *Banking and Business in the Roman World* (Cambridge, 1999).

Archibald, Z., J. K. Davies, V. Gabrielsen and G. J. Oliver (eds), *Hellenistic Economies* (London and New York, 2001).

Archibald, Z., 'Markets and Exchange: The Structure and Scale of Economic Behaviour in the Hellenistic Age,' in Z. Archibald, J. K. Davies and V. Gabrielsen (eds), *Making, Moving and Managing : The New World of Ancient Economies, 323–31 BC* (Oxford, 2004), pp. 1–26.

Bang, P. F., *The Roman Bazaar: A Comparative Study of Trade and Markets in a Tributary Empire* (Cambridge, 2008).

Birley, A., and J. Blake (eds), *The Excavations of 2005–2006*, Vindolanda Research Reports (Hexham, 2007).

Birley, A. R., *Garrison Life at Vindolanda: A Band of Brothers* (Stroud, 2002).

Birley, A. R., 'Some Writing-Tablets Excavated at Vindolanda in 2001, 2002 and 2003,' in *Zeitschrift für Papyrologie und Epigraphik*, 170 (2009), 265–93.

Birley, E., et al., *The Early Wooden Forts: Reports on the Auxiliaries, the Writing-Tablets, Inscriptions, Brands and Graffiti*, Vindolanda Research Reports, New Series, II (Hexham, 1993).

Birley, R., *The Early Wooden Forts: The Excavations of 1973–76 and 1985–89, with Some Additional Details from the Excavations of 1991–93*, Vindolanda Research Reports, New Series, I (Hexham, 1994).

Birley, R., *The Small Finds. Fascicule I. The Weapons*, Vindolanda Research Reports, New Series, IV (Hexham, 1996).

Birley, R., *Vindolanda: Extraordinary Records of Daily Life on the Northern Frontier* (Greenhead, 2005).

Birley, R., *Vindolanda. A Roman Frontier Fort on Hadrian's Wall* (Stroud, 2009).

Bowman, A. K., *Life and Letters on the Roman Frontier* (Avon, 1994).

Bowman, A. K., 'Outposts of Empire: Vindolanda, Egypt and the Empire of Rome,' in *Journal of Roman Archaeology*, 19 (2006), 75–93.

Bourdieu, P., *Distinction: A Social Critique of the Judgement of Taste* (London, 1984).

Cartledge, P., 'The Economy (Economies) of Ancient Greece,' in W. Scheidel and S. von Reden (eds), *The Ancient Economy* (Edinburgh, 2002), pp. 11–32.

Cascio, E. Lo, 'The Role of the State in the Roman Economy: Making Use of the New Institutional Economics' in P. F. Bang, M. Ikeguchi and H. G. Ziche (eds), *Ancient Economies: Modern Methodologies. Archaeology, Comparative History, Models and Institutions* (Bari, 2006), pp. 215–34.

Collingwood, R. G., and J. N. L. Myres, *Roman Britain and the English Settlements* (Oxford, 1936).

Davies, J. K., 'Hellenistic Economies in the Post-Finley Era,' in Z. Archibald, J. K. Davies, V. Gabrielsen and G. J. Oliver (eds), *Hellenistic Economies* (London and New York, 2001), pp. 11–62.

Davies, J. K., 'Linear and Nonlinear Flow Models for Ancient Economies' in J. G. Manning and I. Morris (eds), *The Ancient Economy. Evidence and Models* (Stanford, 2005), pp. 127–156.

Davies, J. L., 'Soldiers, Peasants, Industry and Towns. The Roman Army in Britain. A Welsh Perspective' in P. Erdkamp (ed.), *The Roman Army and the Economy* (Amsterdam, 2002), pp. 169–203.

Driel-Murray, C. van, et al., *Preliminary Reports on the Leather, Textiles, Environmental Evidence and Dendrochronology*, Vindolanda Research Reports, New Series, III (Hexham, 1993).

Duncan-Jones, R., *The Economy of the Roman Empire: Quantitative Studies* (Cambridge, 1974).

Erdkamp, P. (ed.), *The Roman Army and the Economy* (Amsterdam, 2002).

Bibliography

Erdkamp, P., 'Introduction,' in P. Erdkamp (ed.), *The Roman Army and the Economy* (Amsterdam, 2002), pp. 5–17.

Erdkamp, P., 'The Corn Supply of the Roman Armies During the Principate (27 BC–235 AD),' in P. Erdkamp (ed.), *The Roman Army and the Economy* (Amsterdam, 2002), pp. 47–69.

Erdkamp, P., *The Grain Market in the Roman Empire: A Social, Political and Economic Study* (Cambridge, 2005).

Finley, M., *The Ancient Economy*, Sather Lectures (London, 1973).

Finley, M., *The Ancient Economy. Updated with a New Foreword by Ian Morris* (1973; Berkeley and Los Angeles, 1999).

Finley, M., (ed.), *The Bücher-Meyer Controversy* (New York, 1979).

Frere, S. S., *Britannia*, 3rd rev. edn (London and New York, 1987).

Funari, P. P. A., 'The Consumption of Olive Oil in Roman Britain and the Role of the Army,' in P. Erdkamp (ed.), *The Roman Army and the Economy* (Amsterdam, 2002), pp. 235–63.

Greene, K., *The Archaeology of the Roman Economy* (London, 1986).

Harris, W. V., 'Between Archaic and Modern: Some Current Problems in the History of the Roman Economy' in W. V. Harris (ed.), *The Inscribed Economy: Production and Distribution in the Roman Empire in the Light of Instrumentum Domesticum. The Proceedings of a Conference Held at the American Academy in Rome on 10–11th January, 1992* (Ann Arbor, MN; 1993), pp. 11–29.

Hasebroek, J., *Griechische Wirtschafts- und Gesellschaftsgeschichte* (Tübingen, 1931).

Haynes, I., 'Britain's First Information Revolution. The Roman Army and the Transformation of Economic Life,' in P. Erdkamp (ed.), *The Roman Army and the Economy* (Amsterdam, 2002), pp. 111–26.

Hopkins, K., 'Taxes and Trade in the Roman Empire (200 BC–AD 400),' *Journal of Roman Studies*, 70 (1980), 101–25.

Hopkins, K., 'Introduction,' in P. Garnsey, K. Hopkins and C. R. Whittaker (eds), *Trade in the Ancient Economy* (London, 1983), pp. ix–xxv.

Hopkins, K., 'Rome, Taxes, Rents and Trade,' in W. Scheidel and S. von Reden (eds), *The Ancient Economy* (Edinburgh, 2002), pp. 190–230.

Hopkins, T. K., 'Sociology and The Substantive View of The Economy,' in K. Polanyi, C. Arensberg and H. W. Pearson (eds), *Trade and Market in the Early Empires* (Glencoe, IL; 1957), pp. 270–306.

Jones, A. H. M., *The Roman Economy. Studies in Ancient Economic and Administrative History*, ed. P. A. Brunt (Oxford, 1974).

Jones, B., and D. Mattingly, *An Atlas of Roman Britain* (Oxford, 1993).

Mann, J. C., and R. G. Penman (eds), *Literary Sources for Roman Britain* (London, 1996).

Millett, M., *The Romanization of Britain: An Essay in Archaeological Interpretation* (Cambridge, 1990).

Monfort, C. C., 'The Roman Military Supply During the Principate. Transportation and Staples,' in P. Erdkamp (ed.), *The Roman Army and the Economy* (Amsterdam, 2002), pp. 70–89.

Morley, N., *Theories, Models and Concepts in Ancient History* (New York, 2004).

Morley, N., 'The Early Roman Empire: Distribution,' in W. Scheidel, R. Saller and I. Morris (eds), *The Cambridge Economic History of the Greco-Roman World* (Cambridge, 2007), pp. 570–91.

Morris, I., 'Foreword,' in M. Finley, *The Ancient Economy. Updated with a New Foreword by Ian Morris* (1973; Berkeley and Los Angeles, 1999), pp. ix–xxx.

Nafissi, M., *Ancient Athens and Modern Ideology: Value, Theory and Evidence in Historical Sciences* (London, 2005).

Neale, W. C., 'The Market in Theory and History' in K. Polanyi, C. Arensberg and H. W. Pearson (eds), *Trade and Market in the Early Empires* (1957; Chicago, 1971), pp. 357–72.

North, D., 'Markets and Other Allocation Systems in History: The Challenge of Karl Polanyi,' in *Journal of European Economic History*, 6 (1977), 703–16.

North, D., *Institutions, Institutional Change and Economic Performance* (Cambridge, 1990).

Pauly, A., and G. Wissowa (eds), *Paulys Realencyclopädie der classischen Altertumswissenschaft*, rev. edn, vols. I–XXIV (Stuttgart, 1958–80).

Peacock, D. P. S., and D. F. Williams, *Amphorae and the Roman Economy* (London and New York, 1986).

Pearce, J., 'Food as Substance and Symbol in the Roman Army: A Case Study from Vindolanda,' in P. Freeman, J. Bennet, Z. T. Fiema and B. Hoffmann (eds), *Limes XVIII. Proceedings of the XVIIIth International Congress of Roman Frontier Studies Held in Amman, Jordan (September 2000)*, Vol. II, BAR International Series 1084 (II) (Oxford, 2002), pp. 931–44.

Polanyi, K., *The Great Transformation* (1944; New York, 1978).

Polanyi, K., 'Aristotle Discovers the Economy', in K. Polanyi, C. Arensberg and H. W. Pearson (eds), *Trade and Market in the Early Empires* (1957; Chicago, 1971), pp. 64–94.

Polanyi, K., 'The Economy as Instituted Process' in K. Polanyi, C. Arensberg and H. W. Pearson (eds), *Trade and Market in the Early Empires* (1957; Chicago, 1971), pp. 243–70.

Polanyi, K., and C. Arensberg, 'Preface,' in K. Polanyi, C. Arensberg and H. W. Pearson (eds), *Trade and Market in the Early Empires* (Glencoe, IL; 1957), pp. v–xi.

Richmond, I. A., *Roman Britain* (Harmondsworth, Middlesex; 1955).

Rivet, A. L. F., *Town and Country in Roman Britain* (London, 1964).

Rodriguez, J. R., 'Baetica and Germania. Notes on the Concept of "Provincial Interdependence" in the Roman Empire,' in P. Erdkamp (ed.), *The Roman Army and the Economy* (Amsterdam, 2002), pp. 293–308.

Rostovtzeff, M. I., 'Review of J. Hasebroek, *Griechische Wirtschafts- und Gesellschaftsgeschichte* (Tübingen, 1931),' in *Zeitschrift für die gesamte Staatswissenschaft*, 92 (1933), 333–9.

Rostovtzeff, M. I., *The Social and Economic History of the Hellenistic World* (Oxford, 1941).

Salway, P., *Roman Britain* (Oxford and New York, 1981).

Sargent, A., 'The North-South Divide Revisited: Thoughts on the Character of Roman Britain,' in *Britannia*, 33 (2002), 219–26.

Scheidel, W., and S. von Reden (eds), *The Ancient Economy* (Edinburgh, 2002).

Scheidel, W., R. Saller and I. Morris, 'Introduction,' in W. Scheidel, R. Saller and I. Morris (eds), *The Cambridge Economic History of the Greco-Roman World* (Cambridge, 2007), pp. 1–12.

Scullard, H. H., *Festivals and Ceremonies of the Roman Republic* (London, 1981).

Shotter, D., *Roman Britain*, 2nd edn (London, 2004).

Taylor, J., *An Atlas of Roman Rural Settlements in England*, CBA Research Report 151 (Oxford, 2007).

Thompson, E. P., 'The Moral Economy of the English Crowd in the Eighteenth Century,' in *Past & Present*, 50 (1971), 76–136.

Todd, M., *Roman Britain* (London, 1999).

Veblen, T., *The Theory of the Leisure Class* (New York, 1899).

Bibliography

Wacher, J., *Roman Britain* (London, 1978).

Wacher, J., *A Portrait of Roman Britain* (London, 2000).

Ward-Perkins, B., *The Fall of Rome and the End of Civilisation* (Oxford, 2005).

Whittaker, C. R., *Frontiers of the Roman Empire: A Social and Economic Study* (Baltimore, MD; and London, 1994).

Whittaker, C. R., 'Supplying the Army: Evidence from Vindolanda,' in P. Erdkamp (ed.), *The Roman Army and the Economy* (Amsterdam, 2002), pp. 204–34.

Wild, J. P., 'The Textile Industries of Roman Britain,' in *Britannia*, 33 (2002), 1–42.

Williams, D., and C. Carreras, 'North African Amphorae in Roman Britain: A Re-Appraisal,' in *Britannia*, 26 (1995), 231–52.

www.ingramcontent.com/pod-product-compliance
Lightning Source LLC
Chambersburg PA
CBHW061549010526
44115CB00023B/2987